# Girl to Girl

## Heart to Heart Bible Study from Christian Girls

## Laura Elliott, Editor

Publishing Designs, Inc.
Huntsville, Alabama

Publishing Designs, Inc.
P.O. Box 3241
Huntsville, Alabama 35810

Second Printing: June 2006

Printed in the United States

---

Library of Congress Cataloging-in-Publication Data

Girl to girl / Laura Elliott, editor.
    p. cm.
ISBN 0-929540-52-2 (alk. paper)
1. Teenage girls—Religious life. 2. Young women—Religious life.
3. Christian life—Church of Christ authors.
I. Elliott, Laura, 1984-

BV4551.3.G57 2005
248.8'33--dc22
                        2005025067

# Contents

# SECTION FOUR: MORAL ISSUES

## Dedication

To Lydia Edwards—and growing
Christian girls like her everywhere;
we love and appreciate you!

# About the Authors

*G*enevieve Ormon lives in Newport News, Virginia, with her parents, Lloyd and Genevieve. She has a brother, Derrick, and two sisters, Dara and Diona. The Ormons attend the Newport News Church of Christ. Genevieve has taught vacation Bible school, Bible classes, and camp devotionals for girls. She has also spoken at a ladies' day. She has participated in Bible bowls and received awards for Christian leadership and best Bible student at camp. Genevieve enjoys studying history, writing poetry, journaling, drawing, reading, and traveling. She also loves orange cats, neon colors, and would like to live in Nebraska. She was a 16-year-old home schooled junior when she wrote for this book. Her advice to girls is, "Do not say, 'Why were the former days better than these? For you do not inquire wisely concerning this" (Ecclesiastes 7:10).

*L*ora Turner contributed to *Girl to Girl* as a 16-year-old junior at Mars Hill Bible School. She lives in Florence, Alabama, with her parents, Kevin and Cathy, and her two brothers, Garrett and Randall. They all attend the Wood Avenue Church of Christ. She has taught a toddler's Bible class, spoken in chapel to the girls at Mars' Hill, served as a camp counselor, and engaged in stateside mission work. In school Lora is involved in basketball, chorus, and track. Lora hopes to study physical therapy in college. Her favorite movie to quote is *Mulan,* and her favorite Scripture is Colossians 3:23. Her advice for girls is, "Never get so caught up in your life that you don't make time for God."

*H*eather Sparks lives in Mechanicsville, Virginia, where she attends the Cold Harbor Road Church of Christ. Her parents are Joe and Darlene, and she has one brother, William. Heather has taught teen girls' classes, participated in youth activities and Bible bowls, and engaged in stateside mission work. She is studying psychology and chemistry and plans to go to medical school. Heather enjoys reading and playing the guitar. She savors mint chocolate chip ice cream. She enjoys taking women's self defense classes, and she has a deep fear of Wal-Mart. Heather wrote her chapters when she was a 19-year-old sophomore at Virginia Commonwealth University. Her advice to girls is, "Every day has the potential to be better than the last."

*L*yndsay Pierce, a 19-year-old sophomore at Harding University at the birth of this book, is the daughter of Rebecca Palmer and Larry Pierce. She also has an older brother, Mark Pierce. Lyndsay lives in Mechanicsville, Virginia, where she attends the Cold Harbor Road Church of Christ. (At school, Lyndsay attends the West Side Church of Christ.) Lyndsay has been on several mission trips in both the United States and Mexico. She has taught in vacation Bible schools and girls' retreats, served on summer camp staffs, and participated in leadership training for Christ. Lyndsay was graduated from Lee-Davis High School. She is now studying forensic psychology. She is a Resident Assistant in a girls' dorm, and she is a member of Regina (a Harding social club). Lyndsay likes chocolate, the color pink, and also goes by the name, "Piggi." Her favorite Scripture is John 14:1–4, and she advises girls: "Pray continually."

*L*aura Elliott was an 18-year-old freshman at Freed-Hardeman University when she began editing *Girl to Girl*. She is from Mechanicsville, Virginia, where she lives with her parents, Greg and Carolyn, and her brother, Robert. They attend the Cold Harbor Road Church of Christ. Laura has produced a weekly e-devotional for girls, has done camp counseling, and has done mission work in both the United States and Ukraine. She teaches Bible classes and ladies' lessons, as well as working with the Hispanic outreach, at the Estes congregation in Henderson, Tennessee. Laura was graduated from Lee-Davis High School. At Freed-Hardeman, she is studying elementary education, Spanish, and health. Laura enjoys reading, writing, singing, artwork, and crafts. She likes old musicals, and her least favorite animal is the emu. Her advice for girls is, "Make Christianity who you are, and not just something you do."

*H*eather Baker lives in Hoschton, Georgia, where she attends the Jackson County Church of Christ. She added her insight to this work as an 18-year-old freshman at Freed-Hardeman University. Her parents are Ray and Debbie Baker and the late Jan Baker; she has one younger brother, Ray, and two older sisters, Kim and Ashley. She is also blessed with four nieces and two nephews. She has taught Bible classes and participated in Bible bowls. Heather was graduated from Jefferson High School, and is now studying communication and Spanish at Freed-Hardeman. In school, she participates in the Pied Pipers (a children's acting group), Psi Mu (an FHU social club), and the FHU yearbook staff. Heather enjoys the Beatles (and music in general), writing, roller coasters, and laughing till she can't breathe. She advises girls: "Never have ordinary days. Love with all you are every day. Live the fruit of the Spirit."

*H*annah Colley lives in Huntsville, Alabama, with her parents, Glenn and Cindy, and her brother, Caleb. They attend the West Huntsville Church of Christ. Hannah speaks to ladies and girls across the country, and she also participates in Right to Life oratory competitions. She has taken mission trips to New Zealand and Jamaica. Her family has put out three *Hannah's Hundred* CDs, which each have one hundred verses of Scripture set to song for children to learn. Hannah loves mint-chocolate chip ice cream, drama, and classic movies, but she dislikes chemistry. At her drivers' test, she turned on the windshield wipers and left them on the whole time. (It was not raining! She just didn't know how to turn them off!) As a 16-year-old home schooled sophomore at the time of this writing, Hannah's advice to young girls is, "Never give up, girls! Always keep your heart pure and open to God's will!"

*A*llison Boyd wrote her chapters for *Girl to Girl* when she was an 18-year-old freshman at Freed-Hardeman University. She is from McMinnville, Tennessee, where she lives with her parents, Steve and Carol, and her two brothers, Tyler and Daniel. She attends the Bybee Branch Church of Christ. Allison has been involved with Inner Beauty Salon (series of girls' devotionals), Bible Bowl, counseling at camp, and mission work in the United States and Barbados. Allison was graduated from Warren County High School where she played the flute and was a drum major in the band. In college, Allison participates in Missions Group, Psi Mu, Evangelism Forum, the honors association, and the student government. Allison enjoys coffee, sliding down rails, Frank Sinatra, journal writing, and kickboxing. She has a teddy bear named Gustave, and she likes building sandcastles. Her advice to girls is, "Always remember you are beautiful!"

# Preface

As I write this preface, I am lying on a bed in a simple hotel in Arusha, Tanzania (East Africa). I am two weeks into an eight-week commitment to do mission work.

In the past four weeks, 104 souls in the Arusha area have made the decision to put on Christ in baptism. On Friday morning, three men of the Maasai tribe became Christians. Our concern now becomes helping these new Christians stay faithful and go to heaven. One of my friends who studied with some Maasai told me, "Their trouble is they just have so much to give up." Heavy, heavy drinking, polygamy, and animism might top the list.

Really though, don't we all have "so much to give up"? Christ wants us to live completely transformed lives. As young Christian girls, our society screams at us with materialism, impurity, and all kinds of false offers of fulfillment. God wants to offer us something so much better.

Just as Christian Maasai have to live very different from their neighbors, so do Christian girls in America. We must stand out, refusing to fit in with the world so we can fit into the kingdom.

This book aims to help girls stand out. Eight Christian girls worked together to write this book for you. We know that living a transformed life as a young woman can be difficult, but we also know that God equips us with the tools we need to handle the challenge.

As Christian girls just like you, we know that we don't have all the answers, but we would like to share what we have learned as we faced struggles much like yours.

My hope in working with seven of my best friends to write this book is that the book will help young and new Christian girls go to heaven. Just like the 104 new Christians in Arusha, we all have growing, learning, and transforming to do on our way to heaven. As authors we are praying that this book will help do just that for young girls in our Lord's church.

—Laura Elliott, Editor

Dear Girls,

Congratulations on your decision to commit your life to Christ! In doing so, you have heard the word of God (Romans 10:17), believed in Jesus Christ as the Son of God (John 8:24), repented of your sins (Luke 13:3), confessed Jesus Christ as the Son of God (Acts 8:37; Matthew 10:32-33), and been baptized in the name of the Father, the Son, and the Holy Spirit (Matthew 28:19) for the forgiveness of your sins. The Christian life is beautiful and exciting, but it's not always easy. We must constantly be aware of Satan's presence; he is always attempting to take our focus away from God (1 Peter 5:8).

The following lessons are from teenage girls just like you. We all struggle with the issues discussed in this book. However, through Bible study and prayer, we work to overcome them. The Bible is your primary roadmap for life, and this book uses biblical principles to address issues which especially affect teenage girls.

Our prayer is that you will utilize what you learn from this book in your life for Christ.

Love,  Genevieve  Lora  Heather S.
Lyndsay  Laura  Allison
Hannah  Heather B.

# Christian Growth

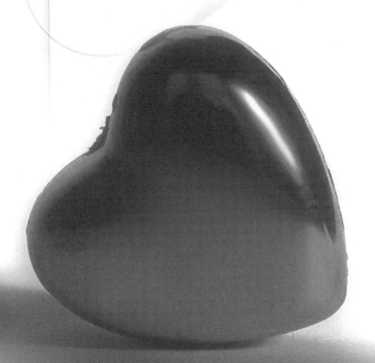

Genevieve Ormon, Lora Turner,
Heather Sparks, and Lyndsay Pierce

# WHAT'S IN THIS SECTION?

# CHRISTIAN GROWTH

## Building a Lasting Commitment to God

Wonderful Words of Life: Bible Study (Genevieve Ormon)

The Privilege of Prayer (Lora Turner)

Spiritual Goals (Heather Sparks)

## Growing with God's People

The Blessing of Christian Fellowship (Lyndsay Pierce)

Getting Involved in the Work of the Church (Lyndsay Pierce)

## Surrounding Ourselves with Support

Friendship Choices (Heather Sparks)

An A-Plus for Christian Education (Lyndsay Pierce)

# CHAPTER ONE

# Building a Lasting Commitment to God

## Wonderful Words of Life: Bible Study

### Genevieve Ormon

*A* legend tells of a little boy who purchased an umbrella. He had been told that this device could keep him from getting wet during a rainstorm. As he headed home in the rain, he confidently held his umbrella under his arm. However, as he was nearing his house he was disappointed because he was drenched! Just as he was ready to discard his new purchase, the wind blew his umbrella open, and he realized that he had to open his umbrella for it to keep him dry!

Many Christians view the Bible in the same way that the boy viewed the umbrella. It lies on their bedside table or travels to worship neatly tucked under its owner's arm. Don't we realize that the Bible, like the umbrella, is useful only to those who open it and carefully look into its pages? (Acts17:11).

> The Bible, like the umbrella, is useful only to those who open it.

The only safe passage through this life is the one illuminated by the light of God's Word.

*And these words which I command you today shall be in your heart. You shall teach them diligently to your children, and shall talk of them when you sit in your house, when you walk by the way, when you lie down, and when you rise up. You shall bind them as a sign on your hand, and they shall be as frontlets between your eyes. You shall write them on the doorposts of your house and on your gates* (Deuteronomy 6:6).

## Lamp unto My Feet

Each time we Virginians get walloped by a hurricane, many in our area experience life for an extended period of time without electricity. Though these times are always ones of inconvenience and much frustration, we always learn valuable lessons from them. As long as it is light outside, life remains normal for the most part. But we have learned through experience to make the most of the daylight hours because when it gets dark, it gets really dark! At night, the only way to move around safely inside or outside is to use some type of light.

In a similar way, the only safe passage through this life is the one illuminated by the light of God's Word. This is why Jeremiah, led by the Spirit, made the statement: "It is not in man who walks to direct his own steps" (Jeremiah 10:23).

On the same note the psalmist penned the words in Psalm 119:105: "Your word is a lamp to my feet and a light to my path." That sounds wonderful, doesn't it? God has promised us that everything we need to get through this life is found in His Word! (2 Peter 1:3).

What happens when we sincerely study the Bible?

❖ We grow to appreciate God's plan (Psalm 119:103).

❖ We grow spiritually (Mark 3:33, 35).

❖ We develop knowledge that we can share with others (Deuteronomy 6:6–9).

❖ We can defend the faith better (Philippians 1:7).

❖ We have great strength during trials, persecution, and discouragement (James 1:2–3; Psalm 119:51; 2 Corinthians 1:3–4).

**Take Time for It! (Psalm 119:97)**

Have you ever been told to do something you really didn't want to do, and upon responding that you didn't have time, were instructed, "Well, you'd better take time for it"? We must apply that kind of discipline to Bible study. We can find time to do the things we want to do!

❖ *Eliminate 30 minutes of television every day.* The time spent watching television can be spent going over passages of Scripture instead.

❖ *Set your clock earlier.* Get up 30 minutes earlier! Are you frustrated over a problem such as low self-esteem, betrayal of trust, or persecution? Do a study on this topic every morning.

❖ *Walk or jog to Scripture.* Get a CD or tape of the Bible. When you exercise, put on your headphones and learn while you work out.

❖ *Memorize Bible verses in the car.* We think nothing of belting out verses to popular tunes. Why not learn the Bible in the same repetitious way?

❖ *Form a support group.* Take turns reminding each other to read and study the Bible. Use notes, telephone calls, and emails to check up on each other.

## TAKE TIME FOR IT

Find a "study-buddy" and choose a book of the Bible to study. Meet in-person or on-line several times a week for 30 minutes. This is a great outreach for a non-Christian friend.

❖ Who will be my study-buddy?

❖ What will we study?

❖ When will we meet?

*Oh, how I love Your law! It is my meditation all the day* (Psalm 119:97).

### Spiritual Starvation

Up to this point we have dealt with some reasons we should study the Bible. Now that we know why we should study, we will go over some suggestions about how to study the Bible effectively.

We need to study regularly (Psalm 119:148, 162; John 4:31–34). None of us would consider it okay to go several days without eating anything. Why? Because, it's just not healthy! Sometimes, though, we are guilty of doing without spiritual meals for several days.

It is sad to think that many Christians are starving themselves to death! We may do just that when we spend days without studying God's Word—and some "Christians" spend weeks without studying. What makes our negligence even worse is that we have a feast before us, served by the Lord Himself! Spiritual nourishment is even more important than physical nourishment. May we never take for granted the welfare of our souls. Be sure to get a nutritious meal every day!

### Tools for Understanding

We have many resources to help us study. Most of us do not have to read the Bible very long before we find a strange or difficult word. Instead of skipping over such words, we can use a Bible dictionary to look them up. Sometimes that task is as easy as flipping to the back of our Bibles to an abridged dictionary. For a more thorough study, many congregations have exhaustive dictionaries in their church libraries.

> Sometimes we are guilty of doing without spiritual meals for several days.

Another resource is a concordance, which lists every passage of Scripture containing a particular word. A concordance is great for doing topical or word studies. For instance, suppose we wanted to study the subject of faith. We could go to concordance and find every passage that contains the word *faith*. A study of these passages would help us to understand the word in its context.

Other good resources to consider are sound commentaries, lexicons, and books discussing Bible topics and principles. We need to be careful about the religious literature we trust. Ask a qualified brother or sister in Christ to recommend sound Christian authors to help you narrow your search. Brotherhood publishers—those noted for publishing sound, doctrinal material—are always glad to recommend literature that will enhance your Bible study.

Organize your Bible study so that you won't let it slip (Ecclesiastes 9:10).

**How to Stay Motivated**

Motivate yourself by studying subjects that interest you. If you are fascinated by the miracles that Jesus and His followers did, do a special study on miracles. While reading a few Scriptures each day is a good way to familiarize ourselves with God's Word, it might not be the best way to gain knowledge and strength. In Bible classes and other public teaching formats, there is usually a selected topic discussed. We are wise to do the same with our personal Bible study.

Journal keeping also makes studying more effective. Keep a special notebook or

## HOW TO STAY MOTIVATED?

Do one or more of the following: visit your church library, visit a neighboring church library, and visit a Christian bookstore. From the information you glean, choose a topic that you feel is interesting.

* Where will I visit?
* What topic interests me?
* When will I do research?

journal set aside for Bible study that can be used to write down Scriptures you read and thoughts that come to you while studying. Later you may revisit some studies that you have completed. Keeping a log of favorite Scriptures is one way to help enhance our personal studies.

**Make It Personal!**

God's Word is our road map for life. If we open our Bibles and study diligently and prayerfully, God will truly bless us. As we look more into God's perfect law of liberty, we will know for ourselves that the Scriptures can truly be called the wonderful words of life (Matthew 4:3–4).

## *The Privilege of Prayer*

***Lora Turner***

You're a Christian! You now have the unique opportunity to have an intimate relationship with God. A most vital part of that relationship is prayer. Prayer is an awesome privilege that God reserves for His children. Through prayer, you can bring your deepest concerns to the Lord. As John tells us, "This is the confidence that we have in Him, that if we ask anything according to His will, He hears us" (1 John 5:14). Prayer is sacred; it must never be taken lightly. The essence of prayer is coming before God humbly and honestly and telling Him what is on your heart. God is so good to us, and He commands that we include Him in our lives and talk to Him. You don't have to use big, fancy words. Just

## MAKE IT PERSONAL

*But be doers of the word, and not hearers only, deceiving yourselves. For if anyone is a hearer of the word and not a doer, he is like a man observing his natural face in a mirror; for he observes himself, goes away, and immediately forgets what kind of man he was. But he who looks into the perfect law of liberty and continues in it, and is not a forgetful hearer but a doer of the work, this one will be blessed in what he does* (James 1:22–25).

talk to God—respectfully!—as you would to a friend because He is the best friend you will ever have. Nothing will enhance your personal relationship with God like daily prayer.

## Too Much to Handle

Many things in life are simply too much for us to handle on our own. God created us to communicate with Him. Prayer can be used in every life scenario. God can help you with anything from arguments with friends, to tests at school, to a friend's or family member's illness. Prayer is especially important when making big decisions. Before Jesus chose the apostles, He spent all night in prayer to His Father (Luke 6:12–13). So whether you're choosing a college, a job, or a mate, always consult God first. Paul instructs in Philippians 4:6 that we should "be anxious for nothing, but in everything by prayer and supplication . . . let your requests be made known to God." Just knowing that God is working in these situations will bring the "peace of God, which surpasses all understanding" to your life (Philippians 4:7).

Nothing is too small to bring before God. Whether it's "God, please keep Dad safe on his way to work," or "God, please give me the opportunity to teach someone today," God appreciates your acknowledgement of His working in your life.

## Take Time

When should we pray? The Bible answers repeatedly: all the time! "Continuing steadfastly in prayer" (Romans 12:12).

## TOO MUCH TO HANDLE

How can I have the peace that passes understanding?

*Nothing will enhance your personal relationship with God like daily prayer.*

## TAKE TIME

### MY PRAYER TRIGGERS

❀ _____

_____

❀ _____

_____

❀ _____

_____

❀ _____

_____

❀ _____

_____

"Evening and morning and at noon I will pray, and cry aloud" (Psalm 55:17). "Pray without ceasing" (1 Thessalonians 5:17). The Book simply speaks for itself. Of course God does not intend for us to go around speaking only prayers. These verses mean that God wants us to focus constantly on Him and the good things He has done for us and can do for us. I know, especially for teenage girls, it can seem hard at times to make time for prayer, but if you just stop and seriously think about what an honor it is to have the ear of the world's Creator at all times, I'm sure your priorities will change!

To help me take time for prayer, I designate certain times and situations that remind me to pray. I call them prayer-triggers. I pray as soon as I wake up in the morning, when I drive by myself, and when I finish a test early. God is so worthy of these recognitions during the day. Prayer should be an on-going joy as you take the opportunity to talk to God.

When I recognize a blessing in my life, I remember to pray. God has done so much for me. My life itself comes straight from Him! It is only appropriate to thank Him. A Christian who is close to God will call on Him in good times as well as bad.

### No Cover-Ups

Prayer is an avenue for confession. Sometimes we try to cover up our faults when we go to God in prayer. Our human nature does not want to admit that we have problems and that we need help. However, submission to that nature defeats the purpose of prayer! God designed prayer so we could bring Him our sins and our difficulties in life and let Him help us through. If you have a problem with cursing, tell God about it. If you are tempted by sexual immorality, tell God about it. If you have trouble being obedient to your parents, tell God about it. Just be open with God. Be willing to confess your sins to Him. First John 1:7–9 tells us that when we, as Christians, confess our sins to the Lord and stop doing them, He will forgive us.

The best thing about prayer is that it works! James tells us in James 5:16 that "the effective, fervent prayer of a righteous man avails much." God knows what is best for us. When we truly trust in Him, He will make "all things work together for good" (Romans 8:28). God is the only being who has unlimited power. Ephesians 3:20 says that our God is "able to do exceedingly abundantly above all that we ask or think." Isn't it incredible that, as a Christian, you have access to that power? If you will ask Him, He will make a difference in your life.

**Not Always "Yes" Answers**

God may not always answer a prayer just the way that we want. Sometimes He says no. (See 2 Corinthians 12:7–9 and Matthew 26:39, 42.) At other times, God may not give us exactly what we want when we want it. But we can rejoice that God knows what we need most (Matthew 6:7–8). He will respond to the needs that we bring to Him in prayer even if He does not do it in exactly the way we wanted or expected.

Your understanding of the power that lies in prayer will grow with time. But the

## No Cover Ups

Practice writing a prayer using the ACTS guide below.

A-doration

C-onfession

T-hanksgiving

S-upplication

❖ How can I express praise and adoration?

❖ What, specifically, should I confess?

❖ Does God bless me? Do I thank Him?

❖ How do I beg God for my desires?

21

best way to learn its power is to practice it daily. Prayer is a blessing, a powerful way to make changes in your life and in the lives of others. Take advantage of it. Tell God everything. Cast all your cares on Him. Try it. You will see that prayer is the answer.

# Spiritual Goals

### Heather Sparks

According to the Merriam-Webster Dictionary, a goal is "an aim or purpose." All of us have goals. If someone were to ask us about our goals for the next ten years, we would probably quickly respond. "I'm going to college," "I'm getting married," and "I'm starting a career" would most likely top that list. However, if someone were to ask us about our spiritual goals, such as what biblical topics or books we plan to study during the next year, would we be able to reply just as quickly? There is certainly nothing wrong with having material goals that will make us more comfortable in life, but we must realize that our spiritual goals will have an effect on where we spend eternity! Let's think some more about our possible spiritual goals and how we can achieve them.

> If someone asks about my spiritual goals, will I be able to reply quickly?

### Prepare Your Hearts

Before setting any goals, we must mentally desire and prepare to accomplish them. So before we discuss our actual goals, we should focus on preparing our hearts. First Samuel 7:3 tells us we should

22

prepare our hearts to serve the Lord. Without prepared hearts, we cannot be the kind of Christians God wants us to be.

Psalm 10:17 expresses God's desire for us to prepare our hearts so we can pray to Him in the proper manner. This adds to the idea of Psalm 119:11, which instructs us to hide God's Word in our hearts in order to keep from sinning. If we lack spiritual knowledge, we cannot have hearts prepared for God, so it is easy for us to fall into Satan's traps. Preparing our hearts is something we must do before we set out to accomplish specific spiritual goals.

**Strive for the Ultimate Goal**

Often the word *strive* is associated with goals. Luke 13:24 tells us that we must "strive to enter through the narrow gate." Living the Christian life is sometimes difficult, but we must remember that we walk the straight and narrow path, the only path leading to heaven (Matthew 7:13–14). Paul speaks a great deal about striving toward our goals. He says in Acts 24:16 that we should "always strive to have a conscience without offense toward God and men." Paul, in Romans 15:30, asked fellow Christians to "strive together with me in prayers to God for me."

While the Bible uses the idea of striving several times, it uses the word *goal* only once. In Philippians 3:14 Paul says, "I press toward the goal for the prize of the upward call of God in Christ Jesus." He alluded to the idea that the Christian life is a race (1 Corinthians 9:24). The prize we should press toward is heaven. Someday we want

## Prepare Your Hearts

Think about preparing for a school exam.

❀ How much time should I study?

❀ What happens if I do not get instructions?

❀ When should I begin to prepare for an exam?

*Then Samuel spoke to all the house of Israel, saying, "If you return to the Lord with all your hearts, then put away the foreign gods and the Ashtoreths from among you, and prepare your hearts for the Lord, and serve Him only; and He will deliver you from the hand of the Philistines"* (1 Samuel 7:3).

How can I commit to prepare my heart for the Lord?

*Girl to Girl*

## WHAT ARE MY GOALS?

Write practical goals under each topic below:

❖ Daily Bible Study

❖ Healthy Prayer Life

❖ Acceptable Worship to God

to say, "I have fought the good fight, I have finished the race" (2 Timothy 4:7).

In Ecclesiastes 7:8 the Bible tells us "the end of a thing is better than its beginning," which is certainly true for a faithful Christian! Experiencing eternity in heaven will be infinitely better than having lived here on earth!

In Psalm 16:8 David said, "I have set the Lord always before me." A goal is often said to be set before or in front of someone, so this statement leads us to believe David spoke of God as a significant part of his goals. In the same manner, God should be at the forefront of the goals we seek to accomplish.

**What Are My Goals?**

The Bible instructs us to set goals and strive to attain them, but what should our goals be, spiritually? And once we have decided what to aim for, how do we successfully achieve these spiritual goals?

❖ *Daily Bible study.* Maintaining a practice of spending time in God's Word daily is difficult for some, no matter how long they have been Christians. However, the Bible commands us to study (2 Peter 3:17–18). If we do not know the Scriptures, how can we know we are living correctly? And how will we know we are teaching others properly? We should follow the example in Acts 17:11 of the Bereans who "searched the Scriptures daily." Once we determine to do so, improving our Bible study habits will not be difficult. Increasing daily study time in small increments—maybe five min-

24

utes a day—will help us reach a speci-fied goal for time spent in regular Bible study. Focusing on a particular chapter or verse or topic in which you are especially interested will help to create a discipline that will bring satisfaction in our study. The more excitement you feel about a Bible verse or topic, the more you will desire to read about it, research its meaning, and make it a part of your life. Studying the Bible is a great way to encourage and edify yourself (Acts 20:32), so it cheers you up as well!

❋ *Healthy prayer life.* A good prayer life does not involve going to God only when we have needs, a mistake people often make. Romans 12:12 is a wonderful verse that demonstrates that we should pray in all things; it implies that prayer gives us hope and rejoicing, as well as patience in the trials we face. Ephesians 6:18 also says we should be "praying always." That is similar to the sentiment expressed in 1 Thessalonians 5:17–18: "Pray without ceasing, in everything give thanks." Second Corinthians 2:14 and Ephesians 5:20 also instruct us to thank God in prayer.

So how can we improve our prayer lives? We can pray during the day if falling asleep while praying at night is a problem, or we can pray while doing menial tasks like driving or cleaning. Do you think your prayers are long? Set a timer. You might be surprised. Prayer is too important to neglect, so be careful not to overlook it.

The more excitement you feel about a Bible topic, the more you will desire to read about it.

## Healthy Prayer Life

### My Weekly Prayer Reminder

❊ **Sunday:** *Saints.* Fellow Christians, church leaders, local congregation, the church universal.

❊ **Monday:** *Missionaries.* Evangelism, missionaries, and the lost (by name).

❊ **Tuesday:** *Teachers.* Bible class teachers, elders, and deacons.

❊ **Wednesday:** *Washington.* Civil government leaders, worldwide peace, spreading of the gospel.

❊ **Thursday:** *Thanksgiving.* Health, food, clothing, shelter, transportation, and spiritual blessings.

❊ **Friday:** *Family.* Friends, and relatives.

❊ **Saturday:** *Shut-ins and Sick.* Elderly and chronically ill. Also the poor, afflicted, and those who mourn.

The June 1994 edition of *Power*, a monthly publication of the Southaven Church of Christ, presented an article by John Tracy, "Practical Suggestions for Prayer." Here are a few of his suggestions that will help improve any Christian's prayer life.

1. Have a prayer list. List people (by name) and church programs for whom/which you want to pray. It is easy to forget if you do not have something to jog your memory.

2. Organize your list. In addition to having general prayers each day and specific prayers for immediate needs, plan a special time to pray for a different subject area each day of the week. (See example in the margin.)

3. Review past prayer lists. This reaffirms our belief that prayer works and increases our thanksgiving.

4. Develop good prayer habits. Spend more time in prayer. Pray at set times every day and be open to opportunities for spontaneous prayer.

❊ *Acceptable worship to God.* Hebrews 12:28 tells us that we must "serve God acceptably with reverence and godly fear." And we should worship as instructed so as not to add to or subtract from God's Word (Revelation 22:18–19). But perhaps most important, we must not seek to please men in our worship, but to please God. Worship is not to be entertainment for us! However, we should be uplifted and encouraged by it, and we should look forward to assembling with Christians. Our attitudes are vitally important to the worship we submit to God.

**Improving My Worship**

So how can we improve our worship to God? Well, we should start by being on time. Tardiness is a common symptom of apathy. Once we arrive, we must focus our minds on the purpose of the assembly. That includes staying awake and alert. The announcements may not seem very important, but missing them often leaves us "out of the loop." We need to know about upcoming activities and those who request our prayers. Then we must engage in all parts of worship in a meaningful way. We must be attentive during the sermon. Take notes. You will have to focus on the sermon to do so. Attentiveness is especially important during the Lord's supper. We are instructed to take it in remembrance of Jesus (Luke 22:19) and the sacrifice He made for us, but how can we concentrate if we are sleepy or distracted? Remembering involves and requires concentration! Worshiping God is a valuable and beneficial activity, and we should strive to be better Christians by first becoming better worshipers.

**Goals for Growth**

The Bible speaks of goals because they are important in our spiritual lives. As we have seen, they are essential to becoming a more faithful Christian. None of us is perfect in our own right and we never will be, so we always have room for improvement.

## IMPROVING MY WORSHIP

### MY REVERENCE DURING THE LORD'S SUPPER

*Therefore whoever eats this bread or drinks this cup of the Lord in an unworthy manner will be guilty of the body and blood of the Lord. But let a man examine himself, and so let him eat of the bread and drink of the cup. For he who eats and drinks in an unworthy manner eats and drinks judgment to himself, not discerning the Lord's body. For this reason many are weak and sick among you, and many sleep (1 Corinthians 11:27–30).*

What is the consequence of using the time during the Lord's supper for frivolous thoughts, rather than remembering Jesus' death, burial, and resurrection?

*Girl to Girl*

## GOALS FOR GROWTH

My Own Spiritual Goal:

How I Will Achieve It:

Of course, our ultimate goal is eternity in heaven with God.

Studying our Bibles daily, praying regularly, and worshiping acceptably are just three of many ways in which we can improve our spiritual lives—ways that help us to grow in Christ. We must set goals in order to grow, and we all want to grow into a life that will continue in heaven.

# CHAPTER TWO

# Growing with God's People

### Lyndsay Pierce

**The Blessing of Christian Fellowship**

A fellowship is a group of people who share common beliefs and companionship. Christians are endowed with the blessing of being a part of a fellowship known as the church. In this fellowship, Christians make lifelong friends who help them grow spiritually and bear their burdens. Additionally, they can have good, clean fun together. Fellowship has a powerful impact on the spiritual growth and strength of a Christian's life!

Fellowship is such a blessing to members of the church. In the New Testament, even the first Christians on the day of Pentecost were in fellowship with one another.

Acts 2:41–47 states,

> Then those who gladly received his word were baptized; and that day about three thousand souls were added to them. And they continued steadfastly in the apostles' doctrine and fellowship, in the breaking of bread, and in prayers. Then fear came upon every soul, and many wonders and signs were done through the apostles. Now all who believed were together, and had all things in common, and sold their possessions and goods, and divided them among all, as anyone had need. So continuing daily with one accord in the temple, and

## THE BLESSING OF CHRISTIAN FELLOWSHIP

What are the benefits of Christian fellowship?

What price do I have to pay to enjoy the benefits?

*Girl to Girl*

## CAN I QUALIFY?

*But if we walk in the light as He is in the light, we have fellowship with one another, and the blood of Jesus Christ His Son cleanses us from all sin* (1 John 1:7).

How does our culture embrace an open-minded attitude about qualifying for the blessings of fellowship?

Contrast the many views that the world broadcasts with the view that the Bible states in Acts 2:38-47.

breaking bread from house to house, they ate their food with gladness and simplicity of heart, praising God and having favor with all the people. And the Lord added to the church daily those who were being saved.

**Can I Qualify?**

How did those on Pentecost qualify for this exclusive fellowship? They repented of their sins, and they were baptized so that their sins could be forgiven (Acts 2:38, 41). Then they not only had fellowship with each other but with God as well, since they praised Him (v. 47). Verse 45 shows that they bore one another's burdens: they shared with anyone who was in need. And they were unified—with one accord (v. 46). This significant passage in Acts illustrates the common beliefs and the companionship of fellowship.

Three blessings associated with Christian fellowship are unity, continual cleansing, and burden-bearing.

❖ *All saints can be united.* "If there is any consolation in Christ, if any comfort of love, if any fellowship of the Spirit, if any affection and mercy, fulfill my joy by being like-minded, having the same love, being of one accord, of one mind" (Philippians 2:1–2).

❖ *The blood of Christ will continually cleanse our sins* (1 John 1:7). When in fellowship, members of the church encourage one another to stay on the heavenly path, hold each other accountable for sins, and encourage repentance unto forgiveness. Christ provides continual cleansing.

❖ *Christians will share one another's burdens.* Galatians 6:2 commands us to "bear one another's burdens, and so fulfill the law of Christ." A Christian does not have to keep her problems and hardships to herself and deal with them alone. A fellowship is a family of believers, and family members help each other! Every mature Christian in the family should support and encourage struggling brothers and sisters in times of difficulty.

**I Need You**

As Christians, we never outgrow the need for fellowship with God's people. We always need each other! Spending time with others who have the same goals and convictions (2 Peter 1:1) and who face the same difficulties will encourage us. The Lord knew what He was doing when He commanded us to take advantage of all the opportunities that we have to worship and fellowship with our brethren! (Hebrews 10:24–25). Since God understands our needs, we can know how right He was when He said, "Behold, how good and how pleasant it is for brethren to dwell together in unity!" (Psalm 133:1).

Young Christian girls in particular can profit from worshiping and spending time with the saints. Many of you may be the only Christian, or one of the few Christians, in your school. That precious time you spend with your brothers and sisters in Sunday worship, Bible classes, gospel meetings, fellowship activities, youth activities, and visiting other congregations will encourage you and help you prepare

## CHRISTIANS WILL SHARE ONE ANOTHER'S BURDENS

Think of two burdens that are common to most teen girls. What can I do to make those burdens lighter?

## I NEED YOU

*Be sober, be vigilant; because your adversary the devil walks about like a roaring lion, seeking whom he may devour. Resist him, steadfast in the faith, knowing that the same sufferings are experienced by your brotherhood in the world* (1 Peter 5:8–9).

What trials have I gone through, only to discover that a new acquaintance had the same experience?

How does having the "same sufferings" bind us together?

for living in the world without being of the world (John 17:15–16).

**Avoiding and Withdrawing**

On the other hand, Christians have to be careful of fellowship in spiritually harmful situations. Members of the church are instructed not to be bound together with unbelievers: "What fellowship has righteousness with lawlessness?" (2 Corinthians 6:14). The answer to such a question is "none"!

If a once-faithful Christian has fallen into temptation and will not return to righteousness, Paul writes that he should be withdrawn from (1 Corinthians 5:1–5). If fellowship is as it should be—an incredible blessing—those living in sin will miss that fellowship when they lose it. The loss should motivate those who are caught up in sin to repent and return to the Lord. However, Paul said in 1 Corinthians 5:13 that until the unrighteous one repents, "put away from yourselves the evil person." Christians are not to fellowship people who will encourage them to abandon the faith.

**Getting Involved in the Work of the Church**

Christian women are vital to the inner workings of the church. They fill a unique role in the promotion of fellowship in the body of Christ. Consider a few examples of service.

❧ *Teach Bible classes or serve as a teacher's aide.* Why not have a goal of learning how to teach from experienced teachers? (Great for teen and preteen girls!)

## AVOIDING AND WITHDRAWING

*But now I have written to you not to keep company with anyone named a brother, who is sexually immoral, or covetous, or an idolater, or a reviler, or a drunkard, or an extortioner— not even to eat with such a person. For what have I to do with judging those also who are outside? Do you not judge those who are inside? But those who are outside God judges. Therefore "put away from yourselves the evil person"* (1 Corinthians 5:11–13).

❧ *Clean and cook.* Help clean the church building or cook for potlucks, shut-ins, and sick people. The encouragement of a young girl can mean the world to someone.

❧ *Send cards to those who are struggling or sick.* You might be the only one who is thinking of them.

❧ *Call members who have not attended worship in a while.* An encouraging word lets fellow Christians know that you care.

❧ *Volunteer for odd jobs.* Assist the church secretary in record-keeping, folding and stamping bulletins, or making copies of Bible class materials.

❧ *Help with vacation Bible school.* Bring friends to hear the message of salvation through Christ. Offer to assist teachers, pass out flyers, or help with special activities.

❧ *Encourage missionaries, members, and friends.* Girls can take mission trips, send cards to missionaries, talk to visitors at church services, and bring friends to gospel meetings.

Without the active participation of Christian women in the church, many people would not be encouraged, helped, taught, or brought to Christ. Their hard work and dedication to the Lord is a great encouragement to the congregation.

**Past and Present Service**

Girls are just as important as boys are, although it may not seem that way in public worship, since women do not preach or lead a prayer or serve the Lord's supper. In

## GETTING INVOLVED IN THE WORK OF THE CHURCH

*Open up your heart and renew your efforts to serve others. Remember, the small things you do can be a big blessing to others (Leading Ladies. p.15).*

*I must work the works of Him who sent Me while it is day; the night is coming when no one can work (John 9:4 ).*

*And whatever you do in word or deed, do all in the name of the Lord Jesus, giving thanks to God the Father through Him (Colossians 3:17).*

*Girl to Girl*

## PAST AND PRESENT SERVICE

Think about my past and present spiritual service:

❉ What excuses have I made for not serving God?

❉ How can I stay motivated to count God in my daily activities?

❉ When is the best time to begin my service to Him?

*For if you remain completely silent at this time, relief and deliverance will arise for the Jews from another place, but you and your father's house will perish. Yet who knows whether you have come to the kingdom for such a time as this?* (Esther 4:14).

1 Timothy 2:11–13, Paul states that women should quietly receive instruction with submissiveness because a woman cannot teach or exercise authority over a man in worship or in the church. Since Christian women are forbidden by Scripture to take an active part in leading worship, some are left dumbfounded, asking themselves, "So what are we supposed to do? Just sit back and let the men do everything?" The answer: "Absolutely not!" Just because there is a limitation on women's involvement in worship, that does not mean we cannot do anything at all! The Bible gives many examples of women's service.

❉ *Many Old Testament women served God obediently.* Proverbs 31:10–31 gives a detailed description of a godly woman. She is a dedicated wife and teaches her children God's commandments with wisdom. She also helps the needy with strength and dignity. But, most of all, she fears the Lord.

Queen Esther, a Jew, risked her life to ask for King Xerxes' help to save the Jewish people from mass murder. (See Esther 4:16.) When the Bible speaks of the kings of both Israel and Judah, often the king's mother is mentioned, showing just how important and influential the mother was to her son. "Then Adonijah the son of Haggith ..." (1 Kings 1:5) is just one example of a king's mother being mentioned in the text. The Old Testament also speaks of prophetesses and a woman judge who were influential in the teaching of God's Word.

- *New Testament women involved themselves in the work of the church.* Acts 9:36 states, "At Joppa there was a certain disciple named Tabitha, which is translated Dorcas. This woman was full of good works and charitable deeds which she did." Tabitha worked in the church by serving others and helping those in need. Lydia's entire household was converted to following Christ (Acts 16:14–15), and she was also hospitable; she invited Paul and Silas to stay with her. In Acts 18:26, Priscilla worked alongside her husband Aquila in privately teaching a man named Apollos the Word of God more accurately. In writing to the church at Rome, Paul says in Romans 16:1–2:

  > I commend to you Phoebe our sister, who is a servant of the church in Cenchrea, that you may receive her in the Lord in a manner worthy of the saints, and assist her in whatever business she has need of you; for indeed she has been a helper of many and of myself also.

  This text illustrates that Phoebe served many Christians and showed hospitality to those, like Paul, who traveled and preached the Word. The New Testament describes many women such as Tabitha, Lydia, Priscilla, and Phoebe, who were involved in the work of the church in the first century.

- *Today's women and girls can be of great service in Christ's kingdom.* Just because Christian women are limited in leadership roles in the church and in the home, that does not mean they cannot do great

## New Testament Women Involved Themselves in the Work of the Church

*So he began to speak boldly in the synagogue. When Aquila and Priscilla heard him, they took him aside and explained to him the way of God more accurately* (Acts 18:26).

What limitations does God place on a woman's role in the church? Give scripture references.

and marvelous things for the Lord! Women can do almost anything, from cleaning the church building to bringing lost souls to Christ. Even the youngest of Christian girls can bring cookies to congregational potlucks and write encouraging notes to peers who do not attend Bible class regularly. Older girls may volunteer to baby-sit for a mother who just needs a night out to relax.

**Girls Are Vital!**

Old Testament women such as Esther and the woman described in Proverbs 31, as well as New Testament women like Lydia and Phoebe, worked daily teaching the way of the Lord. Even today, Christian women have the blessing of ample opportunity to involve themselves in the work of the church. Can you even imagine a fellowship of believers without the vital contributions of women and girls?

**Recommended reading:**

Hampton, Teresa. *Leading Ladies.* Huntsville, AL: Publishing Designs, Inc., 2001.

McWhorter, Jane. *Special Delivery.* Huntsville, AL: Publishing Designs, Inc, 2004.

**Works Cited:**

Hampton, Teresa. *Leading Ladies.* Huntsville, AL: Publishing Designs, Inc., 2001.

# CHAPTER THREE

# Surrounding Ourselves with Support

Heather Sparks and Lyndsay Pierce

## Friendship Choices

**Heather Sparks**

Imagine yourself standing on a chair with someone standing on the floor next to you. Is it easier to pull that person up onto the chair with you or for that person to pull you off the chair? Obviously, it is easier for her to pull you off the chair! This example demonstrates the challenge of being a Christian among worldly friends.

The Bible tells us time and time again to shun evil companions. First Corinthians 15:33 instructs us not to be deceived because "evil company corrupts good habits." We must be careful in choosing our friends. Don't we want to have friends who are not only fun to be around, but those who also share with us the goal of eternity in heaven? In a perfect world, we would all have friends who lead the same, godly lifestyles that we try to live—those who walk the straight and narrow path (Matthew 7:13–14). We all know, however, that the world is not perfect, so we have

> As iron sharpens iron, So a man sharpens the countenance of his friend (Proverbs 27:17).

## FRIENDSHIP CHOICES

*Enter by the narrow gate; for wide is the gate and broad is the way that leads to destruction, and there are many who go in by it. Because narrow is the gate and difficult is the way which leads to life, and there are few who find it (Matthew 7:13–14).*

How do most teens choose their friends? Why isn't the goal of heaven a top priority among most people today?

How do my current friends affect me?

How do other people respond to seeing me with my friends? shocked? impressed? pleased? disappointed?

to make strong efforts to find and develop the right kinds of friendships.

The church is a wonderful place to make friends. Christians are commanded to encourage and edify one another (1 Thessalonians 5:11). What better way to do so than through Christian friendships? We can grow through our Christian friendships with those of all ages. Older and more mature Christians can help us more than we realize!

**Evil Companions**

Our focus is going to be on evil companions and their influence on Christians. Nowhere in the Bible are we forbidden to associate with worldly people; otherwise, how could we evangelize? Jesus commanded us in Mark 16:15 to "go into all the world" in order to spread the gospel. While we are told to go into the world, we cannot allow ourselves to love the world or to be controlled by its influence (1 John 2:15–17).

Worldly associations begin to pose a problem when we compromise our beliefs and morals to suit those of our company. Remember the illustration about being pulled off the chair? Romans 12:2 tells us not to conform to the world, but Christians are often negatively influenced by worldly friends. This is precisely the reason Paul tells us not to be "unequally yoked together with unbelievers" (2 Corinthians 6:14). Of course, we must remember the power of our influence. We are commanded to be examples of Christ and to let our lights shine (Matthew 5:16). Even with our Christian friends, each of us must continue to be "a pattern of good works" (Titus 2:7) and to "abstain from every form of evil" (1 Thessalonians 5:22).

We need to remind ourselves of the consequences of sin. We all know that peer pressure can sometimes be overwhelming, but we should always keep in mind that "the wages of sin is death" (Romans 6:23). Physical death (Proverbs 11:19) and spiritual death (Romans 5:12; Isaiah 59:2) are consequences of sin. Do we really want to endure the consequences of sin because of foolish choices we made while with an immoral friend?

### Excuses for Worldly Associations

❖ *"I am a strong Christian; I won't be influenced immorally.* We may say, "I know the difference between right and wrong," and think that the company we keep has no effect on our lives. But consider the logic of Proverbs 6:27–28. "Can a man take fire to his bosom, and his clothes not be burned? Can one walk on hot coals, and his feet not be seared?"

We are judged by the company we keep, and our friends who know we are Christians have every reason to expect our close associates to be morally pure. Running with friends who "paint the town" every Friday and Saturday night is inexcusable. We must abstain from all appearance of evil (1 Thessalonians 5:22).

But let's go into a part of the real world. Suppose a young Christian has a close relative—a mother, for example— who uses foul language. She might be innocently in line with her mother at

## EVIL COMPANIONS

What are some results you have experienced when you or someone you know has chosen a friend who is evil?

*And do not be conformed to this world, but be transformed by the renewing of your mind, that you may prove what is that good and acceptable and perfect will of God* (Romans 12:2).

What does it mean to be transformed?

How can I be transformed?

How can I use my mind to take myself out of this world?

the grocery store when her mother explodes in a burst of profanity. Every head turns in their direction. The young Christian has little choice about being with her mother. She must make the best of a bad situation. Her purity in life and actions can speak positively for her.

❉ *"They were my friends before I became a Christian, so I can't just ditch them now."* If our non-Christian friends do not accept our beliefs and morals and continue to tempt us to sin, we must end those friendships. Certainly, it is better to lose a couple of friends than to lose our own souls! (Matthew 16:24–27).

❉ *"There aren't any Christians around here."* This excuse is often thrown out as a license to continue bad associations. Finding good Christian friends is becoming increasingly difficult, but that task is not impossible. We are never alone in our Christianity, no matter how much we may feel we are.

Just recall how alone Elijah felt in 1 Kings 19:11–14. He was convinced that he was completely alone in his faith. However, God assured him that was certainly not true. Neither is it the case for us today. We find ways to attend concerts miles from our home. Why not search for youth meetings, camps, and activities where we can make Christian friends? Modern technology shrinks distance to make Christians more accessible.

## EXCUSES FOR WORLDLY ASSOCIATIONS

Common Excuses for Worldly Associations

❉ I feel comfortable around them.

❉ They don't criticize me.

❉ They are popular.

❉ I just want to have fun. Chill!

What are some other excuses for hanging out with kids that do not share our goal of righteous living?

## Two Are Better Than One

Friendship is truly a wonderful thing. Loneliness is not only detrimental to psychological health but to spiritual well-being, too. In Ecclesiastes 4:9, Solomon tells us, "Two are better than one, because they have a good reward for their labor." The labor he speaks of involves helping one another to get to heaven, and it is one of the most rewarding experiences we can have. However, we must remember to use caution in deciding with whom to associate. Quite frankly, choices in friends can mean the difference in eternity.

## An A-Plus for Christian Education

**Lyndsay Pierce**

God has supplied His people with several networks of support to help them grow spiritually. Fellowship with followers of Christ, including friends and family, is just one of these networks. However, one of the most influential networks in a young adult's life is her education.

Christian young people can receive a quality education at one of several colleges or universities associated with the Lord's church. Of course, we understand that not all Christian girls will be able to attend a Christian school because of financial situations, family obligations, or the location of the school. Young Christian girls can still make an outstanding impact for Christ through employment or in a state school or in whatever they choose to do, as long

## TWO ARE BETTER THAN ONE

Find an example of a model friendship in the Bible. What characteristics make this friendship a good one to imitate?

Contrast Christian qualities and non-Christian qualities in friendships. How do these qualities affect friendship?

## AN A-PLUS FOR CHRISTIAN EDUCATION

COUNT YOUR BLESSINGS!

How can a Christian education be a blessing in the following areas?

❁ Knowledge

_____

❁ Faith

_____

❁ Encouragement

_____

❁ Good Influence

_____

❁ A Circle of Believing Friends

_____

as they are committed to staying faithful to the Lord. However, if a girl desires a Christian education, she should explore every avenue that will aid her in attaining that goal. What about a work program or scholarship opportunity or loan assistance? Ask, ask, ask!

A Christian university gives young women wonderful opportunities! The following blessings of Christian education make it a worthwhile choice:

❖ *It is a blessing to grow in knowledge of the Word.* Through daily Bible classes, chapel, devotionals, and classes taught from a Christian perspective, students constantly learn about God's Word. In Proverbs 4:13, Solomon writes: "Take firm hold of instruction, do not let go; keep her, for she is your life." Christians should embrace the opportunity to learn more since the whole duty of man is to fear God and keep His commandments (Ecclesiastes 12:13). Solomon continues to write that God's instruction, knowledge, and wisdom far surpass the value of silver, gold, and precious jewels (Proverbs 8:10–11). In the New Testament, the apostle Paul instructs in Colossians 3:16: "Let the word of Christ dwell in you richly." A university affiliated with the church will offer opportunities that encourage students to dig deeper into God's Word on a daily basis. Knowledge accumulated in the university environment will make a lifetime impact.

Girls who are seeking to enroll in a Christian college should carefully evaluate available colleges. Not all schools

> What about a work program, scholarship opportunity, or loan assistance? Ask, ask, ask!

that associate themselves with the Lord's church stand for biblical teaching in every area, and so girls need to ask questions, do research, and, if possible, make campus visits in order to determine if the school is one in which they really can grow.

❋ *It is a blessing to strengthen one's faith.* Regarding Paul's second missionary journey, Acts 16:5 states, "So the churches were strengthened in the faith, and increased in number daily." Just like Paul's teaching, the teaching at the university will strengthen the student's faith and help bring the lost to Christ. Besides the daily Bible classes, chapel, fellowship, and devotionals, one unique opportunity that Christian universities provide is mission work. Several universities provide opportunities for foreign mission work in dozens of countries, as well as many opportunities in the United States. Leading others to Christ is a wonderful way to strengthen one's faith.

❋ *It is a blessing to be encouraged by fellow Christian students.* In Romans 1:12 Paul speaks to the saints in Rome of such encouragement: "That is, that I may be encouraged together with you by the mutual faith both of you and me." Both professors and students will strengthen their faith because of the overwhelming amount of love for the Father displayed while achieving a Christian education.

❋ *It is a blessing to be able to avoid a worldly, sinful influence.* In some state universi-

## IT IS A BLESSING TO STRENGTHEN ONE'S FAITH

*Receive my instruction, and not silver, and knowledge rather than choice gold; for wisdom is better than rubies, and all the things one may desire cannot be compared with her (Proverbs 8:10–11).*

How could it be that a person might have a great education without having pursued wisdom?

## IT IS A BLESSING TO BE ENCOURAGED BY FELLOW CHRISTIAN STUDENTS

What Bible character was called "the son of encouragement"? Why?

How can I be like him?

## It Is a Blessing To Be Able to Avoid a Worldly, Sinful Influence

*Therefore do not let sin reign in your mortal body, that you should obey it in its lusts. And do not present your members as instruments of unrighteousness to sin, but present yourselves to God as being alive from the dead, and your members as instruments of righteousness to God (Romans 6:12).*

## It Is A Blessing To Gain A Circle Of Believing Friends

If I choose to go to college, what will I look for in a college?

What will be the most important factor in deciding where I go to school?

ties, drugs, alcohol, and premarital sex run rampant among the students. Fewer students will dabble in these sins at a Christian university. Romans 6:12–13 records Paul's warning to Christians not to let sin reign in them or present themselves as instruments of unrighteousness. Followers of Christ should flee from sin. Since a Christian woman should present her body as a living and holy sacrifice to God, she should not be conformed to the world. Christian universities strive to keep even the appearance of evil from their students in order to keep their minds focused on obeying and pleasing God; therefore, they will help Christians flee sinful desires.

❧ *It is a blessing to gain a circle of believing friends.* Who will support your walk with God? Proverbs 18:24 speaks of a friend who sticks closer than a brother. Such a Christian friend is willing to help you at all costs.

This type of friendship is also very desirable in a husband. Many young women will marry men they meet in college. So a school that attracts faithful Christians might be a priority for a Christian girl. This does not mean that every young man who attends a Christian school is a potential husband for a godly girl! But it may be that she will meet a faithful Christian man during this time or through the network of friends that she establishes in college.

**Set Your Heart to Study**

It is wonderful that more and more teenagers are considering a college education. Young Christian women who plan on going to college need to consider prayerfully all the benefits of attending a university affiliated with the church. While achieving a Christian education, a young lady has great opportunity to strengthen her faith, flee from temptation, and—who knows—maybe even gain lifetime Christian friends! Christian girls should emulate Ezra's eagerness to learn more about God's commandments: "For Ezra had prepared his heart to seek the Law of the Lord, and to do it" (Ezra 7:10).

## SET YOUR HEART TO STUDY

What are some ways a Christian can serve the Lord if she chooses to attend a state university or a community college?

**Recommended reading:**

McWhorter, Jane. *Friendship: Handle with Care*. Nashville, TN: Gospel Advocate Co., 2002.

# NOTES

# Self-Fulfillment

Laura Elliott and Heather Baker

WHAT'S IN THIS SECTION?

# SELF-FULFILLMENT

## Searching for Happiness

Laura Elliott

## Becoming a "Perfect Ten" in God's Eyes

Heather Baker

# CHAPTER FOUR

# Searching for Happiness

## Laura Elliott

We all want to be happy! Everybody likes to feel important and loved. These facts hit home for me when I searched on Amazon.com to find out just how common are concerns about happiness. I found over 40,000 books when I searched with the word "happiness." Over 80,000 came up under "meaning of life." People are searching! They want a meaningful life—one filled with purpose. I decided to modify my Amazon.com search to cover specifically teenage girls. Would you believe that still 11,000 books came up on "teenage girls and self esteem" and 5000 came up for "teenage girls and overcoming depression"?

We all know why, don't we? We all have friends who seem to have everything they need or could want, and yet, they are not happy. Many girls—even young Christians—struggle with really having lasting happiness. Yet, this searching is not new. Someone in the Bible faced a similar struggle long before any of us did. King Solomon wrote, "I searched in my heart . . . till I might see what was good for the sons of men to do under heaven all the days of their lives" (Ecclesiastes 2:3). See, Solomon searched for happiness too! Let's go back to the book of Ecclesiastes and retrace his steps. Let's learn together

> We all have friends who seem to have everything, and yet, they are not happy.

## SEARCHING FOR HAPPINESS

Read Matthew 5:3–12. What characteristics does Jesus link with happiness?

## WISDOM

*Happy are the people whose God is the Lord!* (Psalm 144:15).

If I dedicate more time to scholastic achievement than I devote to spiritual development, how will this affect my soul?

from Solomon where to look—and where not to look!—in order to be happy.

❖ *Wisdom.* As a young king, he asked God for wisdom (1 Kings 3:5–12), and the fact that God gave it to him shows that knowledge is worthwhile (James 1:5). The wisdom God gave Solomon excelled even the knowledge of the wisest in the cultures around him (1 Kings 4:30–34). Throughout the books of Proverbs and Ecclesiastes, Solomon demonstrated that he did understand the importance of knowledge. Yet, he also understood that knowledge is not the magic key to happiness.

We start to build on the wrong foundation when we expect wisdom to bring us everything. AP exams, SATs, ACTs, GPAs, and similar tests are important, but they are also not everything!

Solomon finally came to understand that "in much wisdom is much grief" (Ecclesiastes 1:18) and that "much study is wearisome to the flesh" (12:12).

❖ *Work.* He really made many remarkable accomplishments! Solomon built the temple of the Lord, the king's palace, a special home for one of his wives (1 Kings 9:15, 24), the wall of Jerusalem, and several cities (1 Kings 9:15–18). Our text in Ecclesiastes even adds that he made vineyards, orchards, and irrigation systems (2:4–6). Not only that, but Solomon also spoke 3000 proverbs and 1005 songs (1 Kings 4:32). Solomon knew what it meant to do something and to do it well! He had success as far as the world saw, yet he felt something was missing.

We dream of great accomplishments too; we all wish for some measure of the world's success in our lives. During high school we try to achieve by volunteering and becoming involved in clubs or after-school projects. Or we want to be the best player on our sports teams. Some of us have jobs, and we spend time there. We should try to accomplish much! All of these things are great achievements and worth having in our lives! But none of them alone will ultimately make us happy.

When Solomon reflected on his work, he said,

> I looked on all the works that my hands had done and on the labor in which I had toiled; and indeed all was vanity and grasping for the wind. There was no profit under the sun (Ecclesiastes 2:11).

Solomon called all these earthly successes "vanity." That means uselessness, emptiness, and frustration! Solomon knew that eventually he would have to leave all his work to someone else (2:18–20). He understood that while his accomplishments were valuable, earthly success could not bring spiritual happiness!

❖ *Riches.* Sometimes we look for happiness in riches. We have all been caught up in the race to have the coolest stuff first—whether CDs, clothes, money, or maybe even a car. Solomon had "silver

## WORK

Find Bible verses that speak of building my hopes on things that will not make me happy. Compare these to the previous passage from Matthew 5:3–12. Where do I turn in order to find happiness?

What are some of the behaviors of a "workaholic"?

How can work hinder my salvation?

## PLEASURE

*I said in my heart, "Come now, I will test you with mirth; therefore enjoy pleasure"; but surely, this also was vanity . . . Whatever my eyes desired I did not keep from them. I did not withhold my heart from any pleasure, for my heart rejoiced in all my labor; and this was my reward from all my labor. Then I looked on all the works that my hands had done and on the labor in which I had toiled; and indeed all was vanity and grasping for the wind. There was no profit under the sun* (Ecclesiastes 2:1, 10–11).

"If only_____
_____, I would be happy!"

List several "if only" statements that you have observed from others.

How do these "if only" statements remind you of Solomon's searching?

and gold and the special treasures of kings" (Ecclesiastes 2:8). He passed all the earth's kings in riches (2 Chronicles 9:22), and he made silver as common as stones in Jerusalem during his reign (1 Kings 10:27). But what did he say about it? "Riches are not forever" (Proverbs 27:24). In other words, once again he had to say, "It's not out there; happiness can't be found in the world!"

❧ *Pleasure.* Sometimes, instead of work or wisdom or riches, we want to try worldly pleasure for happiness. How many times have you heard girls say (or maybe even thought yourself), "I wish I had a boyfriend" or "I wish I were more popular"? Lots of girls think clothes, movies, popularity, drugs, and especially boys can make them happy.

When Solomon started experimenting with how to find happiness, he said in his heart, "Come now, I will test you with mirth; therefore enjoy pleasure" (Ecclesiastes 2:1). As Solomon searched, he said, "I did not withhold my heart from any pleasure" (2:10). See, Solomon tried it all—wine (2:3), rich entertainment, music, "the delights of the sons of men" (2:8), and sex (1 Kings 11:1–3). Solomon would have known if any of these things brought lasting happiness! But, instead, he "said of laughter—'Madness!'; and of mirth, 'What does it accomplish?'" (Ecclesiastes 2:2).

Girls, good friends are wonderful, but you won't find happiness in any boy or in being popular. You are special without them too! God loves you (John 3:16). He made you in His own image (Genesis 1:26–27), sent His Son to die for you (Galatians 2:20), and made all spiritual blessings available to you (Ephesians 1:3). Can you imagine being more loved and special than that? The Creator of the whole universe cares about you (1 Peter 5:7) and wants you to be happy in the real riches that only He provides (Ephesians 3:8).

**Fulfill Your Purpose**

For all his searching, did Solomon ever find happiness? What did he conclude? Fortunate for us, he did find the answer. Ecclesiastes 12:13, the next to last verse in the book tells us: "Let us hear the conclusion of the whole matter: Fear God and keep His commandments, for this is man's all."

Solomon found out what it means to be happy! He discovered the real purpose of life and what it really means to have a life. It means to serve God with everything we have! The rest of the Bible teaches the same message. We have abundant living in Christ! (John 10:10). We have the peace that passes all understanding (Philippians 4:7). We have a purpose in Christ and an incredible peace and happiness that comes from fulfilling that purpose!

Girls, you are special, wonderful, and beautiful! The Lord thinks so; He made you that way! He wants you to be happy. Jesus promised us peace—a peace unlike any the world offers (John 14:27). Jesus also wants us to have joy—happiness (John 15:11). Because God wants us to be happy, He has given us the resources we need to have

## FULFILL YOUR PURPOSE

*Let us hear the conclusion of the whole matter: Fear God and keep His commandments, for this is man's all* (Ecclesiastes 12:13).

*This Book of the Law shall not depart from your mouth, but you shall meditate in it day and night, that you may observe to do according to all that is written in it. For then you will make your way prosperous, and then you will have good success* (Joshua 1:8)

*He who would love life and see good days, let him refrain his tongue from evil, and his lips from speaking deceit, let him turn away from evil and do good; let him seek peace and pursue it* (1 Peter 3:10–11).

From the previous verses, how does the Bible define true success?

What is my definition of true success?

happiness. He tells us in His Word that we do not have to waste time looking in the world for wisdom, work, material riches, or worldly pleasure. Jeremiah 9:23–24 says,

> Thus says the Lord: "Let not the wise man glory in his wisdom, let not the mighty man glory in his might, nor let the rich man glory in his riches; but let him who glories glory in this, that he understands and knows Me, that I am the Lord."

God tells us that we can be happy by fulfilling our "all"—our purpose—by fearing Him and obeying His commands.

# CHAPTER FIVE

# Becoming a "Perfect Ten" in God's Eyes

Heather Baker

When we as young women look around us, it is difficult to determine who or what we should strive to be. We see conflicting views of today's successful woman. Should she be a hard-core career woman, a bustling mother, or a charming lady? There are no reliable answers to this question if we look for the answer in this world; each person would have us to believe something different! If we truly desire to develop into a godly Christian woman, we must consider first and foremost the Scriptures, the source of all trustworthy solutions. When we strive to be what God would have us to be, His opinion is the only one that matters. So what does God have to say concerning the godly woman?

> When I strive to be a Christian girl, God's opinion is the only one that matters.

## The Role-Model for Women

One of the best known Scriptures concerning godly women is Proverbs 31, a passage of truth that describes the "virtuous [honorable] woman." However, this biblical basis of womanhood may seem outdated to many. Some may ask, "What did Solomon—the man who penned the book of Proverbs—know about women, espe-

## THE ROLE-MODEL FOR WOMEN

How can I increase my faith that God made me and God knows me?

Think of woman's complexity. Did I arrive in life with an "operating manual"?

When the Creator gives me instructions regarding the best way to live, how do I regard those instructions?

## HER WORTH IS FAR ABOVE RUBIES

Why is buying beauty a dangerous practice?

cially women living in the twenty-first century?" We must remember that Solomon's words came from God. In light of this observation, the more appropriate question is, "What does God know about women?" When we look at it this way, we can see just how much wisdom the thirty-first chapter of Proverbs can impart to us. Because God created woman (Genesis 2:18–24), He knows everything about us and can provide us with a long-lasting description of what a woman should be. I encourage you to read and study the entire passage on the virtuous woman. But for now, let's look at a handful of the statements within the passage and see how they relate to the modern woman. After all, if we want to develop into godly women, we must begin applying principles of Proverbs 31.

❈ *Her worth is far above rubies* (v. 10). The society in which we have grown up highly esteems some women because of their material wealth. After all, money is what can buy fancy clothes, "miracle" ointments, pricey make-up, and cosmetic surgery. It seems that money can buy beauty for anyone. But buying beauty is a dangerous practice. Because we can so readily buy beauty, we tend to base a person's worth on her physical features rather than what is inside her—her real self. Although this statement seems trite and clichéd, it is true. How many times do we find ourselves drawing conclusions about a person before we speak a word to her? And on what are these conclusions often based? That's right: physical appearance. According to God's

Word, the worth of a godly woman is far above the worth of any material possessions. This means that a woman need not possess clothes in the latest fashion or have a wrinkle-free face to be virtuous. If we can learn this lesson while young, we will be ahead of the game.

Being able to look beyond a person's physical appearance and find what is on the inside is most certainly a sign of social and spiritual maturity. After all, it is God who gives us the ability to get wealth (Deuteronomy 8:18). Without our God-given abilities, none of us would have anything. When we can base our own character and our perceptions of those around us on non-physical things, we are well on our way to virtuous womanhood.

❧ *And willingly works with her hands* (v. 13). Let's face it, girls: a little hard work never hurt anyone. If we want to get anywhere in life, we must be willing to put our comfort aside for a while. This applies to anything we may wish to do with our lives. Ask any woman who has climbed the corporate ladder or successfully reared her children; she will tell you there were times when she poured everything she had into a project. Many times it is hard to make ourselves begin the difficult work, but once we do, we find that it pays big dividends. God knows human nature, and He knows it is hard for us to give ourselves completely to the work at hand. Fortunately, He reassures us with His presence. Second Chronicles 15:7 says,

## HER WORTH IS FAR ABOVE RUBIES

*Do not look at his appearance or at the height of his stature, because I have refused him. For the Lord does not see as man sees; for man looks at the outward appearance, but the Lord looks at the heart* (1 Samuel 16:7).

If I read the previous verse, "For the Lord does not see as the teen girl sees, for the teen girl looks at the outward appearance, but the Lord looks at the heart," how does this make me feel?

## AND WILLINGLY WORKS WITH HER HANDS

*Whatever your hand finds to do, do it with your might; for there is no work or device or knowledge or wisdom in the grave where you are going* (Ecclesiastes 9:10).

*Let him who stole steal no longer, but rather let him labor, working with his hands what is good, that he may have something to give him who has need* (Ephesians 4:28).

Why does God instruct me to work with my hands?

What are some practical ways young girls can begin serving others?

How can I "willingly work with my hands" and yet avoid seeking happiness only through my work?

"But you, be strong and do not let your hands be weak, for your work shall be rewarded!"

Surely Noah leaned on God's sure presence when he underwent the task of building a massive ark. Likewise, Abraham knew God was with him when he obeyed God's command to sacrifice Isaac, his son. Without God, these men could not have accomplished their noble deeds. It is both humbling and encouraging to remember that the Bible characters were human—no more, no less. Do you realize what this means? This means that we have every bit as much opportunity to work hard and succeed as they did. What an encouraging thought! We are protected and supported by God just as they were. Ladies, let's begin working hard now, for our work will be rewarded.

❊ *The heart of her husband safely trusts her* (v. 11). We need to be trustworthy in all of our relationships. Trust is a deep emotion, rooted in action. It is the ability to leave something in someone's hands and know that it will be taken care of. If you plan on marrying one day, today is the day to begin making yourself trustworthy. Trust involves more than a confidence that our spouse is faithful to us. It is the knowledge that you have an unfailing source of support and that your spouse will do his best. Trust is especially important in dealing with finances in a family and is even more important when children come along. Trust is the foundation of any relationship. We can start preparing ourselves for this now by being trustworthy daughters, sisters, and friends. We can begin by purging sins, such as gossip, from our lives and completing tasks assigned to us.

❋ *She extends her hand to the poor, yes, she reaches out her hands to the needy* (v. 20). A virtuous woman looks beyond her own needs to the needs of others. It is easy when we are focused on physical things to think only of what we do not have. When we compare ourselves to others, we think we simply must have what everyone else has. Yet, when we begin purchasing those things, we only find ourselves more unfulfilled. However, if we focus on spiritual things, we begin to realize that we do not need what everyone else has to be happy. In fact, the more we have, the more we have to worry about. Instead of thinking of our own needs, we should start looking at those around us. So many people are in much worse condition than we ever thought of being.

Note this statement by Alan Bryan:

> If our income is more than 500 dollars per year, economically we are among the upper ten percent of this world's population, as far as wealth. Our wealth is so abundant that if we have more than one room in which to live, electric lights, running water (especially hot and cold running water), radio, television, and any kind of car to travel about in, we are in the upper three percent of the world's population as to wealth *(Climb Happiness Hill)*.

## THE HEART OF HER HUSBAND SAFELY TRUSTS HER

Think of someone you trust. How many of the following areas does that trust include?
___ Love
___ Loyalty
___ Secrets
___ Children
___ Money

## SHE EXTENDS HER HAND TO THE POOR, YES, SHE REACHES OUT HER HANDS TO THE NEEDY

Why do we usually think of the needy in terms of physical needs? Why should I focus also on the spiritually needy?

*Let each of you look out not only for [her] own interests, but also for the interests of others* (Philippians 2:4).

How can I reach out to the physically and spiritually needy with my time as well as my money?

How many people do I know who are truly reaching out to the needy? Am I?

## HER CHILDREN RISE UP AND CALL HER BLESSED

*But seek first the kingdom of God and His righteousness, and all these things shall be added to you* (Matthew 6:33).

How does society pressure girls to focus on career rather than family?

How does a career-focus endanger the likelihood of "children rising up and calling her blessed"?

In the back of our minds, we know the statement is true, but there is a difference between knowing it and feeling it. However, it is not until we meditate on it and truly put ourselves in the other person's shoes that we recognize how much God has blessed us.

To be truly honorable, we must spend some time fulfilling needs that are not ours. Jesus is the perfect example of a giving spirit. Having nowhere to lay His own head, He went about teaching and healing others. He truly put His own comforts aside in service to His fellow man, even to the point of death. We know this and yet we do not act upon it. Service does not have to involve some grand and glorious task. As Desmund Tutu said, "Do your little bit of good where you are; it's those little bits of good put together that overwhelm the world." If we all do our part, starting now, the world cannot help but improve.

Let us remember that if we truly want to be like Jesus, we must be servants. Being servants now can lead us to greater lengths of service as we mature.

❖ *Her children rise up and call her blessed; her husband also, and he praises her* (v. 28). What a wonderful opportunity that God has given women to be the queens of their own homes through their influence as wives and mothers! Let us remember also that the noblest position we can hold is that of the Christian wife and mother. We must not let the world degrade women who choose to be stay-at-home moms or housewives. No one makes more difference in a person's life than his wife and mother, especially if the wife and mother fear God.

Our society sends us conflicting messages about our role as women. We come to understand that we can climb the corporate ladder and have remarkable careers. And we can! However, if we make the choice to marry and have children, God's Word lays down some clear expectations about our responsibility to our families. We must choose to honor God's wisdom above pursuing worldly goals at the cost of our families! (Matthew 6:33).

Titus 2:4–5 tells young women "to love their husbands, to love their children, to be discreet, chaste, homemakers, good, obedient to their own husbands, that the word of God may not be blasphemed." Our society will not tell us that mothers have a role more important than a career, but God who knows best tells us loudly and clearly: today's homes need mothers in them!

Young Christian girls should dream of fulfilling their God-given role if they plan to have children. God does not want us to pass off the responsibilities—and wonderful joys and privileges!—of being a wife and mother to someone else so that we can pursue worldly goals. He wants us to pursue heavenly goals and to be present to help train our children towards heaven too.

## WIVES AND MOTHERS

*The older women likewise, that they be reverent in behavior, not slanderers, not given to much wine, teachers of good things— that they admonish the young women to love their husbands, to love their children, to be discreet, chaste, homemakers, good, obedient to their own husbands, that the word of God may not be blasphemed* (Titus 2:3–5).

From the previous verse, it is easy to see that the older women are to admonish the young women. How does this go against our culture today?

Where do young women usually seek counsel when they encounter relationship problems with men, children, mothers-in-law, parents, siblings, and friends?

Where do I seek help with my problems?

> The best way to ensure our success as godly women is to realize what is important now!

### Nothing Else Matters

Proverbs 31:30 sums up the main idea of the entire passage: "Charm is deceitful and beauty is passing, but a woman who fears the Lord, she shall be praised." Girls, the most important thing in our lives is to fear the Lord; nothing else matters as much—not clothes, not cars, not boyfriends—nothing. Although these things often play an important role in our lives, they are not what will get us to heaven. So exactly what type of women should we be? We need not spend years searching for our purpose in life; God has told us why we are here. Ecclesiastes 12:13 says, "Let us hear the conclusion of the whole matter: Fear God and keep His commandments, for this is man's all." Because we already know our purpose, we can spend these young adult years developing the skills we need to become women of God.

We can be godly women as long as we keep God first and remember that our main goal is to serve Him. The best way to ensure our success is to start realizing what is important now! Let's make it a point to pray every day that we may keep our focus on what is really important—developing our spiritual lives according to the pattern set by God's Word.

### Works Cited:

Bryan, Alan. *Climb Happiness Hill*. Birmingham, AL: Christian Development Institute, 1978.

# Doctrinal Issues

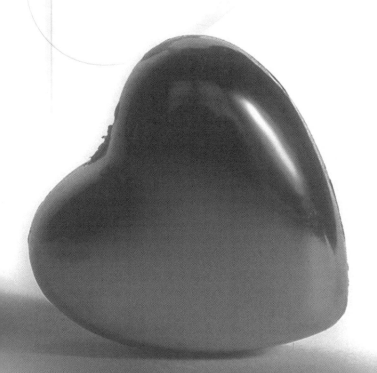

Laura Elliott

# WHAT'S IN THIS SECTION?

## DOCTRINAL ISSUES

### Fighting Evolution

Laura Elliott

### Offering Meaningful Worship in Song

Laura Elliott

# CHAPTER SIX

# Fighting Evolution

## Laura Elliott

Nearly two thousand years ago, Paul, by inspiration, exhorted the young Timothy to "fight the good fight of faith" (1 Timothy 6:12). This challenge required Timothy's strength and devotion, just as it requires the strength and devotion of faithful young people today. The church today needs us to fight this good fight, and the Lord still requires that we do.

I remember my ninth grade year of high school clearly. In health class, we learned about vestigial organs—supposedly unnecessary body parts that developed millions of years ago for the survival of our primitive ancestors. Then, in world history, we talked about the dawn of man, the time before humans had "fully developed." And maybe most frustrating of all was biology. Four long chapters of our textbook covered nothing but evolution!

Young Christians today will face evolution in school. They need to expect it and know how to combat it. What can be more important to our souls than defending the faith and standing for truth?

*What can be more important to our souls than defending the faith and standing for truth?*

### Victims of Evolutionary Process?

The rest of this chapter is a result of my research from my ninth-grade search for

## Victims of Evolutionary Process?

In the following verses, underline things that I am to avoid as I try to fight the good fight of faith:

*Nor give heed to fables and endless genealogies, which cause disputes rather than godly edification which is in faith . . . But reject profane and old wives' fables, and exercise yourself toward godliness . . . He is proud, knowing nothing, but is obsessed with disputes and arguments over words, from which come envy, strife, reviling, evil suspicions, useless wranglings of men of corrupt minds and destitute of the truth, who suppose that godliness is a means of gain. From such withdraw yourself* (1 Timothy 1:4; 4:7; 6:4–5).

the truth regarding evolution. I could not bear sitting in a class listening to a teacher tell us that we did not have a Creator! I could not stand hearing that we were nothing more than highly developed animals! That line of reasoning has led many young people to believe we are not valuable or special. That philosophy gives us no reason to care about right and wrong. Why should we, if we are just accidental victims of an evolutionary process that did not have us in mind at the beginning?

I wanted to challenge my teachers. They sounded so historical and so scientific. Still, I knew that true history and true science would not conflict with the Bible. Paul told young Timothy to avoid the opposition of "profane and idle babblings and contradictions of what is falsely called knowledge" (1 Timothy 6:20). Many lessons that I heard from my ninth grade teachers were not scientifically accurate at all. But to most of us they sounded like they were. I had to study on my own to find scientific material in support of creation, but I definitely found it.

**Creation, Not Evolution**

This chapter cannot contain all the scientific research that supports creation. There is just too much! However, this chapter should motivate you to go out and research the subject on your own. Study the specific topics your classes mention and then be ready with a biblical answer (1 Peter 3:15). Don't let your teachers go unchallenged when they tell valuable and impressionable young people that they came from nowhere, have no God-given purpose, and are going nowhere.

What does Christianity offer that evolution cannot?

❊ The greatest story of love (Ephesians 5:2)

❊ A place in the greatest institution—the church! (John 8:24; Luke 13:3; Matthew 10:32; 1 Peter 3:21; Acts 2:47)

❊ The best law that man has ever known (Deuteronomy 10:12–13)

❊ Inner peace (Philippians 4:7)

❊ A sense of worth (2 Peter 3:9)

❊ An eternal home (2 Timothy 4:8)

Certainly, many other reasons exist for choosing God over evolution. Not doing so will bring on the greatest punishment. God's Word extends the greatest invitation, provides a solution to the greatest sickness, and supplies the truth in times of weakness. On and on the list might go. The list of the condemned in Revelation 21:8 includes the unbelieving. Obedience to the truth will pay great rewards; rejecting it will result in eternal punishment.

**The Bible: A Perfect Scientific Record**

The Bible will not agree with every aspect of man's science because "the world through wisdom did not know God" (1 Corinthians 1:21). Because God has created the universe and knows more about it than man does, everything He has revealed in His Word about it is accurate. Here are a few examples of scientifically accurate facts in the Bible:

## CREATION, NOT EVOLUTION

*But the cowardly, unbelieving, abominable, murderers, sexually immoral, sorcerers, idolaters, and all liars shall have their part in the lake which burns with fire and brimstone, which is the second death* (Revelation 21:8).

Why are the unbelieving linked with the cowardly, murderers, and other sinful people?

❖ *The earth is round.* The first well-noted European voyage around the entire world began in A.D. 1522. That Magellan voyage proved beyond any doubt to European skeptics that the earth is round. A great Bible prophet had penned that fact centuries before, in Isaiah 40:22, where the inspired writer speaks of "the circle of the earth."

❖ *The earth hangs freely in space.* The mythology of some ancient cultures reflected the belief that the earth rested on the shoulders of one of their gods. We now know that the earth rotates on it axis, freely suspended in its orbit. The Bible has proclaimed that fact since times of old. In Job 26:7, the writer exalts the God who "hangs the earth on nothing."

### Theistic Evolution

Jon Gary Williams, in *The Other Side of Evolution* (p. 57), explained theistic evolution as an attempt to believe the Bible and evolution at the same time. Theistic evolutionists believe that God used evolution to fill the earth with living creatures. Many of my teachers have said that God created the first life and then allowed that simple life to evolve into many complex species. Those teachers thought their philosophy would keep everybody happy, that the compromise would satisfy their students who believe in creation. And many students did accept this teaching because it allowed them to straddle the fence. However, in an attempt to believe the Bible and evolution at the same time, the theistic evolution-

> Theistic evolutionists believe that God used evolution to fill the earth with living creatures.

68

ist faces several great challenges from the
Genesis account of creation.

The account in Genesis tells us that
God created all fully developed plant and
animal life, including man, in six days
(Genesis 1:31–2:2). Evolution holds that
fully developed life took many millions of
years. In an attempt to harmonize the two
contradictory ideas, theistic evolutionists
teach that each creative day spanned millions of years. In so doing, those evolutionists ignore the fact that the Bible says that
one evening and one morning made up
each day (Genesis 1:5, 8, 13, 19, 23, 31).
The Bible uses singular nouns: "evening"
and "morning." This statement leaves no
room to think that the creation days lasted
any longer than a normal day—just one
evening and one morning.

Note the problems between evolution
and the biblical account of creation:

| In the Bible . . . | In Evolution . . . |
| --- | --- |
| Life produced young after its kind (Genesis 1:11, 12, 21, 24, 25). The Bible speaks of the creation of fully developed animals and plants. | Life gradually changes with new generations. Life developed from lower life forms. |
| Man came from the dust of the ground (Genesis 2:7). | Man came from a primitive creature that evolved into man. |
| Animals also came from the ground (Genesis 2:19). | Animals came from some primitive life form. |
| God made man and woman separately (Genesis 2:22). | Man and woman evolved during the same time period. |

## THEISTIC EVOLUTION

Why does it take faith to accept the theory of evolution?

How is that kind of faith any different from faith in the creation theory?

How does agreement with the theistic evolutionist compromise the Word of God?

Theistic evolution ultimately fails to combine God's Word with evolution and come away with both intact. Agreeing with the theistic evolutionist requires compromising the Word of God. Many theistic evolutionists have tried to justify the compromise by saying that the first 11 chapters of Genesis tell a mythological story or that they do not give a literal account. Notice the inconsistency of those who take the position that Genesis 1–11 does not give an accurate account:

❀ Exodus 20:11 and 31:17 refer to the literal six-day creation period.

❀ Mark 13:19; Ephesians 3:9; 1 Timothy 4:3; and Revelation 4:11 all refer to God as the Creator.

❀ Romans 1:20 and 2 Peter 3:4 both speak of the creation.

❀ First Corinthians 11:9 and 1 Timothy 2:13 draw facts from Genesis 2:21–22 as Paul speaks of the role of woman in the church.

❀ Hebrews 11:4 confirms the historical existence of Cain and Abel as recorded in Genesis 4:4–5.

❀ Genesis 5:3–32 gives the same genealogies that Luke 3:36–38 does. Since Luke gives a true account, so must Genesis.

❀ Genesis tells of Enoch in Genesis 5:22–24. Hebrews 11:5 confirms this statement as truth.

A rejection or misconstruction of the first 11 chapters of Genesis leads to a rejec-

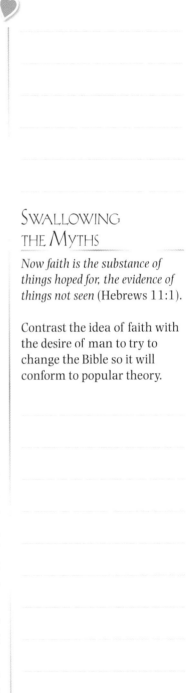

tion or misconstruction of the better part of the rest of the Bible! Theistic evolution fails to provide an alternative to creation. Christians must simply accept what the Bible teaches without trying to change it to conform to every new idea of man.

### Swallowing the Myths

Students must completely research the material used in public education as support for evolution. Many people have swallowed myths that discredit God as the divine Creator. They are familiar with the material that evolutionists use to support their beliefs, but they have never researched it or examined it to determine its reliability. Young Christians sometimes begin to feel that evolution has scientific support and no one can fight against it. That is not true! Such a mindset comes from fear, but "God has not given us a spirit of fear, but of power and of love and of a sound mind" (2 Timothy 1:7).

Biology teachers often leave out information—sometimes ignorantly, sometimes intentionally—when presenting their evolution lessons. The scientific support for evolution has big gaps! While evolutionists cannot prove their theory, they often appear to do so through skillfully prepared lectures—add a little here and take away a little here; distort the facts! Evolutionists are masters at delivering distorted information, misconstrued to their own liking. They often omit information that is detrimental to their pet theories, accepting only that which seems profitable to them. Students who will not devote extra time to learning the truth are in danger of falling

## SWALLOWING THE MYTHS

*Now faith is the substance of things hoped for, the evidence of things not seen* (Hebrews 11:1).

Contrast the idea of faith with the desire of man to try to change the Bible so it will conform to popular theory.

for a concept that does not have true scientific backing.

### "Missing Links" Myth

For example, students learn of many discoveries that some have called missing links. The "prehistoric man"—the supposed link between modern man and a lower form of life—is used as an example of a missing link. Some eager students conclude that man must have evolved from lower life forms, since scientists have supposedly found missing-link fossils. However, the scientists have failed to announce that many of these missing links come from just a few bones *(The Other Side of Evolution,* p. 45). Students do not research these missing links enough to know that evolutionists have constructed entire creatures from these few bones without having any way of knowing how the creature truly appeared. Students are not normally told about the many times that evolutionists have announced a missing link, only to discover that its link turned out to be a true human or a true non-human, but never anything in between *(The Other Side of Evolution,* p. 46). Scientists cannot substantiate the claim of evolution with any legitimate missing links! (See *The Other Side of Evolution,* pp. 45–52 for further information on missing links that have turned out to be completely human or completely non-human.)

Most teachers present the geologic time table or the fossil record as absolute proof for organic evolution. However, they do not readily admit that no real evidence for intermediate or partially developed life forms

> Scientists have failed to announce that many missing links come from just a few bones.

72

has been found. Neither do they admit that
the fossil record reveals complex life forms
at the lowest levels of the table *(The Other
Side of Evolution,* p. 42; see also *The Mythology of Modern Geology,* pp. 17–20). The
fossil record frequently reveals fossils out
of their evolutionary order. Many areas on
earth do not have some fossil that we expect them to have. Other areas have fossils
in reverse order, the "older" fossils being in
the upper layers with the "younger" fossils
in the lower layers. (Wayne Jackson shows
the many problems of the evolutionists'
fossil record and geologic time table in *The
Mythology of Modern Geology.*)

**"Age of the Earth" and "Horse Evolu-
tion" Myths**

Another example of unresearched
material that many students accept comes
when dealing with the age of the earth.
When looking in the right material, a student can find scientific information that
supports a young earth, as supported by
the Bible, and not the old one demanded by
evolutionists. (See *The Creation-Evolution
Controversy,* pp. 159–177; see also "The
Young Earth.")

Textbook charts compare baby humans
to baby chickens and illustrate "horse evolution." The careful student knows that the
original artists of some of those evolutionary drawings admittedly drew their dia-
grams inaccurately. The same student also
knows that the charts of so-called "horse
evolution" face challenges. As a matter of
fact, no intermediate links exist between the
horses. Archeologists have even found evidence of horse species that still live today in

## "MISSING LINKS" MYTH

Make a list of spiritual
questions that evolution fails
to answer, such as "What is
man's purpose?"

Make a list of scientific
questions that evolution fails
to answer, such as "What is
the source of the first matter?"

## "AGE OF THE EARTH" AND "HORSE EVOLUTION" MYTHS

Why are people so quick in believing evolutionary theories such as "horse evolution" and so reluctant in believing "God said"?

How can I help other young people turn to the Bible to determine origins rather than embracing the theory of evolution?

the same geologic layers with extinct horses, when many years supposedly existed between them *(The Creation-Evolution Controversy,* p. 301). Such information defies the old age of the earth concept, the concept of evolution, or both! The horses from the "horse evolution" idea come from many different parts of the world *(The Other Side of Evolution,* p. 43). Scientific evidence has failed to support the idea that these horses have evolved in the way that the chart illustrates. The evolutionist has no right to use such an ungrounded argument as evidence for his evolutionary beliefs.

### "Vestigial Organs" Myth

In anatomy and health classes, students are taught that humans have degenerate organs that do not serve any known function. Those organs are called vestigial organs—small, degenerate, imperfectly developed organs passed down to us from our ancient ancestors. However, the teacher will not usually remind the students that just because man does not know the function of an organ, that does not mean the organ has no function. Nor is the teacher likely to inform the students that the body does not use all of its structures at the same time or for the same purpose; children or growing infants may need one organ during development, while as they grow older, that organ becomes less crucial *(The Other Side of Evolution,* p. 35). As science has progressed, scientists have discovered that some organs once called "useless," "left-over," "vestigial," or "extra" have some purpose *(A Study Course in Christian Evidences,* p. 66). For example, scientists now know that the appendix and tonsils fight infection (*The Other Side of Evolution*, p. 397) whereas before they considered these organs to be useless.

## Blind Guides

Students have to monitor closely what they hear, learn, and choose to believe. Many teachers have never researched evolution with an honest heart, seeking to know whether it is wrong or right. Therefore, many students have spiritually blind teachers. Jesus warned, "And if the blind leads the blind, both will fall into a ditch" (Matthew 15:14). Students stand in danger of falling eternally if they allow the words of a blinded teacher to guide them. The lies of evolution are everywhere, but the truth still remains in God's Word. A grave danger lies in accepting the words of a teacher without researching them. The Bible still reveals all truth and it plainly teaches: God created all, and nothing has evolved into existence!

## Battle Strategy

An army cannot successfully fight a battle without a plan or a strategy. By the same token, Christian youth today need some idea of how they can fight the good fight of faith. Here are some ways:

- ❋ By living in such a way that we show Christianity in a positive light (Philippians 2:15).

- ❋ By teaching the way of truth (Ezra 7:25).

- ❋ By filling our minds with the truth (Hosea 4:6).

## BLIND GUIDES

Why is it a good idea for me to memorize the following verse?

*For what if some did not believe? Will their unbelief make the faithfulness of God without effect? Certainly not! Indeed, let God be true but every man a liar* (Romans 3:3–4).

Underline the previous verse. Transfer it to a note card and read it each day this week.

## BATTLE STRATEGY

My Battle Strategy:

❀ Ask questions in class.

❀ Present evidence for creation—or against evolution—in class.

❀ Host a Bible study after school for girls who want to learn to defend the truth of the Bible.

❀ Suggest to the elders that the middle school and high school classes study creation and science in their Bible classes.

❀ Sign up for web mail that keeps you current on scientific issues:
www.apologeticspress.org
www.christiancourier.org

❀ By objecting publicly to false doctrine (Ephesians 5:11).

What about you? How can you fight the good fight of faith against the erroneous theory of evolution? One of the best things you can do is arm yourself, first with God's Word and then with scientific knowledge that shows the accuracy of the Bible. You will probably not be the only one in your science classes who does not believe in evolution. Your willingness to research and defend creation may make an eternal difference for others. They probably want to believe the Bible too, and they need to hear you stand up and courageously defend it.

You can and you must do something! May God bless us all in fighting the good fight of faith!

**Works Cited:**

Jackson, Wayne. *The Mythology of Modern Geology.* Stockton, CA: Apologetics Press, 1980.

Thompson, Bert. "The Young Earth." Montgomery, AL: Apologetics Press, Inc., 1994.

Thompson, Bert and Wayne Jackson. *A Study Course in Christian Evidences.* Montgomery, AL: Apologetics Press, Inc., 1992.

Williams, Jon Gary. *The Other Side of Evolution.* Lavergne, TN: Williams Brothers Publishers, 1996.

Wysong, R. L. *The Creation-Evolution Controversy.* Midland MI: Inquiry Press, 1976.

# CHAPTER SEVEN

# Offering Meaningful Worship in Song

### Laura Elliott

The youth rally began with the song leader's instructions. "Everyone repeat after me: I am glad that you are here. And, the only reason I am here is to worship God." Then the PowerPoint flashed up the words to the song, "I Belong to Jesus." As soon as he started the song, the group began singing and clapping out the beat. They swayed with the music, danced to its beat, and added enthusiastic cheers at the end of each line of song.

Several months later, another group of young people gathered late at night. They too sought to worship God. The young people stood for an hour in a crowded chapel as the young men among them took turns leading songs. Some closed their eyes in concentration. But something was different. Among this group, no one chose to clap or dance; no one cheered during the lines of the song. The young people lifted their voices to proclaim, "There is a God; He is alive!" and "I will serve no other God. Lord, I'm here to stay."

What separates these two groups? I observed both of them, and I believe that each group wanted to worship God in a

*They swayed with the music, danced to its beat, and added enthusiastic cheers.*

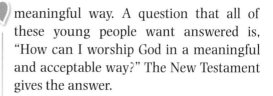meaningful way. A question that all of these young people want answered is, "How can I worship God in a meaningful and acceptable way?" The New Testament gives the answer.

## OFFERING MEANINGFUL WORSHIP

Underline the phrases in the following scripture that apply to my attitude in worship. Circle the blessings of obedience.

*Honor Him, not doing your own ways, nor finding your own pleasure, nor speaking your own words, then you shall delight yourself in the Lord; and I will cause you to ride on the high hills of the earth, and feed you with the heritage of Jacob your father. The mouth of the Lord has spoken (Isaiah 58:13–14).*

### God, the Center of Worship

The mighty God says, "I am the Lord, that is My name; and My glory I will not give to another" (Isaiah 42:8). He calls on His people to recognize that He alone is the focus during worship! God does not want us to concentrate on how we can make worship more fun! In so doing, we would honor our own preferences above God's commands and take away from the honor we should give to Him. Even an angel refused to accept worship for himself in Revelation 22:8–9. He made it clear who worship is really about when he said simply, "Worship God."

In the days of the Old Testament, many of God's people took the focus off God during worship and turned the focus to themselves. God sternly corrected them: "When you fasted and mourned . . . did you really fast for Me—for Me? . . . do you not eat and drink for yourselves?" (Zechariah 7:5–6). When God saw that people wanted to make their acts of devotion about themselves rather than about Him, He was not happy with their offerings!

In Isaiah 58 God gave His people a recipe for enjoyment in worship. The Israelites were engaged in ungodly lifestyles, doing what they wanted to do, thus making their worship unacceptable.

First, God told them that if they wanted to enjoy worship, they must stop "doing your pleasure on My holy day" (Isaiah 58:13). God reminded His people what worship is all about—Him. Even today we cannot add to our worship societal trends and personal desires to entertain and still present worship that is acceptable to God.

God also told His Old Testament people that if they would enjoy worship, they must "call the Sabbath a delight, the holy day of the Lord honorable" (Isaiah 58:13). While the New Testament does not bind the keeping of the Sabbath, we can still follow the principle of this verse. We can still learn to call God's worship a delight. We can determine that we will enjoy worshiping in the way God has instructed. We do not worship to entertain ourselves or to have fun, but God says that we can still find worship enjoyable if we will do it in His way.

God promised that when we "shall honor Him, not doing your own ways, nor finding your own pleasure, nor speaking your own words, then you shall delight yourself in the Lord" (Isaiah 58:13–14). As we consider what pleases God and what does not, we must remember that worship is not our opportunity to entertain ourselves. Rather, it is our opportunity to pour out our souls in reverence to God. Since God is the center of worship, He has the right to tell us what kind of worship He wants!

## God, the Commander Regarding Worship

Why do we need to discuss God's commands about worship in a book for teen girls? Think back to the two worship scenes at the beginning of this chapter. Most young people want to worship God, and in

## GOD, THE CENTER OF WORSHIP

*The death of Christ did away with the Mosaical Law with all its hundreds of rules and regulations. The new covenant was to be different. A simple, heartfelt religion was to replace the pomp and pageantry of the temple. Hopefully, the people had matured spiritually to the point that they themselves could come wholeheartedly before the throne of God, realizing that he was the one to be praised in the manner of his choice whether they understood his reasons or not. The people were now to be participants instead of spectators* (We Bow Down, p.128).

How do most teens regard their status in worship—as spectators or as participants?

What kind of responsibility does being a participant (not a spectator) in worship place upon me?

## GOD, THE COMMANDER REGARDING WORSHIP

What are "psalms, and hymns, and spiritual songs"? Consider this answer:

*These describe the lyrics of approved music. Psalms are scripture set to music. Hymns are songs of praise to God. Spiritual songs describe those which are designed around spiritual themes and which motivate singers and listeners to greater spiritual service* (Words of Truth, *vol. 34, no. 48, p.2*).

many places we can find worship that looks like one of these two scenes. Young people need to know how to worship according to God's commands!

God commands us to sing when we come before Him in worship. Let's look at two important verses about singing:

> Let the word of Christ dwell in you richly in all wisdom, teaching and admonishing one another in psalms and hymns and spiritual songs, singing with grace in your hearts to the Lord. (Colossians 3:16)

> Speaking to one another in psalms and hymns and spiritual songs, singing and making melody in your heart to the Lord. (Ephesians 5:19)

God makes clear what He requires of us in song. Every New Testament reference to singing refers only to singing. He wants us to do just that without adding our own ideas to it. If an English teacher assigns a research paper, her students will not expect to get credit for turning in poems or outlines. Why not? After all, the teacher did not say that poems and outlines were unacceptable. But she made her expectations clear by telling the students what she wanted.

God operates in the same way. Through His Word, He tells us what He wants—singing. He does not have to add a list of everything He does not want. Revelation 22:18–19 specifically warns:

> For I testify to everyone who hears the words of the prophecy of this book: if anyone adds to these things, God will add to him the plagues that are written in this book; and if anyone takes away from the

words of the book of this prophecy, God shall take away his part from the Book of Life, from the holy city, and [from] the things which are written in this book.

## Worship Is Not Entertainment

God wants us to obey His commands just the way they are! In every biblical example of Christians worshiping—and other historical accounts, as well—Christians sang in reverence to God, but did not add anything to that singing. When we add instruments, clapping, or cheering to our worship, we add those things for our own entertainment rather than for God's pleasure. After all, God who tells us how to worship never gives us permission to add those things to our singing.

We must remember that how we act at a concert and how we act in worship are not the same! After all, we do not go to worship for entertainment.

The verses we have studied show us how to test our singing to see if it pleases God. Our singing must . . .

❖ Honor God as the focus of worship (Revelation 22:9).

❖ Be vocal (Ephesians 5:19).

❖ Create melody in the hearts of the worshipers (Ephesians 5:19).

❖ Teach and admonish (Colossians 3:16).

Just as instruments cannot meet these four requirements, neither can clapping, dancing, or cheering.

# WORSHIP IS NOT ENTERTAINMENT

### GETTING MY HEART RIGHT!

*God is Spirit, and those who worship Him must worship in spirit and truth* (John 4:24).

*The Pharisees could teach us one of the most important lessons of all. We can carry out commands to the letter of the law and yet be completely displeasing in the sight of God. We may engage in congregational singing of scriptural songs, without the aid of mechanical instruments of music . . . and our worship will still be unacceptable if our hearts are not right. While it is necessary to spend time in warning about false teaching, we must constantly be on guard concerning our attitudes. We could win the battle and yet lose the war* (We Bow Down, p. 143).

How is it possible to have the right music and still give God the wrong worship?

## No Jazz Necessary

How can I become more aware that God is the audience for our worship? What Bible examples reinforce my answer?

### No Jazz Necessary

God understands our desire to worship Him, and He understands the joy that most of us have in music and song. For that reason, He has made singing a part of worship. Young people can learn to enjoy worshiping God's way. They should be insulted by the idea that worship has to be "jazzed up" or modernized in order to satisfy them.

Think about some popular trends in church music and evaluate them on the following chart.

Spiritually minded young people recognize the arrogance of assuming we know how to worship in a way better than the way God has authorized. May God bless us all as we try to participate in worship in a meaningful and satisfying way that pleases Him!

| Is this activity . . . | YES | NO |
|---|---|---|
| Focused on God, rather than a group of people or a person (Revelation 22:8–9)? | | |
| Singing (Ephesians 5:19)? | | |
| Creating melody in the hearts of all the worshipers (Ephesians 5:19)? | | |
| Teaching and admonishing (Colossians 3:16)? | | |

**Works Cited**

McWhorter, Jane. "Heart Song," *We Bow Down*. Huntsville, AL: Publishing Designs, Inc., 2002.

*Words of Truth*, "Special Music in the Church—Ephesians 5:19," Glenn Colley (Jasper, Alabama: Sixth Avenue Church of Christ) vol. 34, no. 48.

# Moral Issues

Laura Elliott, Heather Sparks, Hannah Colley,
Lora Turner, Lyndsay Pierce, and Allison Boyd

# WHAT'S IN THIS SECTION?

# MORAL ISSUES

## Choosing Entertainment

Can't I Ever Have Any Fun? (Laura Elliott)

Influence of Entertainment (Heather Sparks)

## Avoiding the Drug Scene

Alcoholic Beverages (Hannah Colley)

Why You Should Just Say No! (Lora Turner)

Talking the Talk (Hannah Colley)

## Dating and Waiting

Where, Oh Where, Is Mr. Right? (Lyndsay Pierce)

Hello, Purity Lover! (Allison Boyd)

## Dressing for Spiritual Success— What the Guys Say

Allison Boyd

## Dancing Out of Step

Hannah Colley

CHAPTER EIGHT

# Choosing Entertainment

## Laura Elliott and Heather Sparks

## Can't I Ever Have Any Fun?

*Laura Elliott*

"What do you do for fun?" A friend asked me this question near the end of my senior year of high school. You might have been asked that question too. Perhaps you choose not to watch some of the movies your friends watch. Maybe you will choose, or have already chosen, not to attend your senior prom, not to go to certain parties, and not to go after graduation to party at "Beach Week." In the next few chapters, we will discuss these and other choices. But as the world looks on and sees us pass up certain activities, sometimes we do hear, "What do you do for fun?"

After all, many people do look at the Bible and say, "That's just rules, rules, rules! If you're a Christian, there's a whole list of things you can't do. You can't ever have any fun!" We need to understand how to respond when people make these and other observations, and we should know that as Christians we can be the happiest people ever, rather than the most boring and saddest!

### CAN'T I EVER HAVE ANY FUN?

If you are happy, notify your face! Since I am a Christian, why should I be joyful, rather than always looking sad?

Find a Bible example of someone who became a Christian and was joyful.

## Joy vs. Rules

The New Testament emphasizes the blessings and the joy of Christianity. In fact, it refers to joy and rejoicing four times more often than it refers to sorrow and sadness! Peter wrote to the early Christians:

> Though now you do not see Him, yet believing, you rejoice with joy inexpressible and full of glory, receiving the end of your faith—the salvation of your souls (1 Peter 1:8–9).

Christians can rejoice because of the salvation of their souls! Peter describes that joy as inexpressible. Christians cannot fully explain that kind of joy to non-Christians. The world's definition of fun does not even begin to approach the real peace (Philippians 4:7) and confidence (Ephesians 3:11–12) that Christians have about the things that really do matter.

Yet, some people will still complain about "rules, rules, rules." Does the Bible have restrictions? Yes! For example, we are not to "continue in sin" (Romans 6:1), and the Bible does list many activities as sin. (See 2 Timothy 3:1–5.)

Well, does Christianity really require that much of us? Again, yes! God expects us to turn our lives around and live in complete dedication to Him (2 Corinthians 5:17). Christians will not do some things people in the world do for fun, and the world will think that is strange (1 Peter 4:3–4). So there are commands and sacrifices bound on Christians. Our attitude about God's Word will determine whether or not we live with respect to these commands and still have a joy-filled life.

> Christians will not do some things people in the world do for fun.

After all, John said, "For this is the love of God, that we keep His commandments. And His commandments are not burdensome" (1 John 5:3). Along similar lines, Jesus said, "For My yoke is easy and My burden is light" (Matthew 11:30). These verses do not mean that Christianity is always a walk in the park. However, they do teach that Christian living is not a miserable existence with impossible rules!

**God Commands; God Knows Best**

Deuteronomy 6:24 does an outstanding job of explaining why God gives commands at all. It says,

> And the Lord commanded us to observe all these statutes, to fear the Lord our God, for our good always, that He might preserve us alive, as it is this day.

God wants only our best interests! Why did He give commands about the way we treat our bodies? He wants us to live strong healthy lives. Why did God give commands about sexual purity? He hates to see us have broken hearts, unhealthy bodies, and overwhelming situations. God gives commands for our good (Deuteronomy 10:12–13). Even when we do not understand the reason behind a command, we obey it out of respect for our God whom we trust knows best!

**Give It Up!**

As we cover the next few chapters, examine each activity with an open Bible and an honest heart. Think of sin as something you want to give up. After all, Christ gave up so much for you! Giving up certain

## JOY VS. RULES

*Therefore, if anyone is in Christ, he is a new creation; old things have passed away; behold, all things have become new (2 Corinthians 5:17).*

Congregations in Jamaica sing, "The things I used to do, I don't do them no more," and "The places I used to go, I don't go there no more." The title of the song is "Great Change." Why does becoming a new creature involve a great change?

How does Christianity cause rejoicing?

activities as we come to understand they do not please God is not a horrible sacrifice of all our fun. Instead, it is something we will naturally want to do when we have our hearts in the right place (1 John 5:3).

Keep in mind that of course sin looks fun! Satan makes it look very attractive (Genesis 3:6). If sin did not seem fun, then no one would do it! So we need to keep in mind that there is such a thing as good, clean fun too. I live on the campus of a Christian college, and I see people having good fun all the time! Whether it's playing Frisbee in the commons—or maybe even the auditorium—or listening to students play guitar and keyboard in the student center, there are ways to have fun without feeling guilty about it later. Our lives overflow with simple joys to help us have real fun.

As we study together, let's resolve to find what God wants us to do and then do it according to His Word. When we make that commitment, we will be able to enjoy the life God has given us and have fun in a way that does not hurt the Lord.

## Give It Up!

Make a list of music, shows, and movies that you enjoy and that are appropriate for Christians. What about them appeals to you?

## Influence of Entertainment

**Heather Sparks**

As Christian girls living in the twenty-first century, the media constantly surrounds us with immorality. Bombarded with television shows, commercials, movies, music, and magazines, it seems as if we cannot escape. What kind of influence do these negative sounds and images have on today's audiences? Is it true that such media blitz is unavoidable, or is there something we can do about it? Let's examine the influence of today's so-called entertainment and explore some solutions to this ever growing problem.

Let's think about what goes on in these media sources. On television, profanity and other foul language is prevalent, as are immodesty and portrayals of violence and stereotyping. Almost every sitcom and drama on television these days portrays at least one openly homosexual character; premarital sex and adultery are flaunted. Smoking and drinking are portrayed positively and perceived by most as cool. Even television commercials, once intended only for advertising, are becoming increasingly filthy. Companies advertising alcoholic beverages target young audiences, because they realize teenagers are often more susceptible to marketing campaigns. Not only do television and commercial advertising glamorize the drinking of alcohol, but movies do as well.

Movies, including those rated PG and PG-13, often contain violence, nudity, foul language, and sexual situations. We can find out specifically why a movie has its particular rating by using a popular parental screening site, www.screenit.com. Upon some examination of recent movies, it is astounding how much profanity, sexuality, and general crudeness even the PG movies contain! With the help of the "screenit" website and some sound judgment, those who wish to make better decisions about which movies to view can do so.

## INFLUENCE OF ENTERTAINMENT

When I go to www.Screenit.com, I can reevaluate my personal CD and movie collections. Why is it important for me to get rid of anything that is inappropriate?

Who controls what goes into my mind?

## CALLING NAMES

*Love suffers long and is kind; love does not envy; love does not parade itself, is not puffed up; does not behave rudely, does not seek its own, is not provoked, thinks no evil; does not rejoice in iniquity, but rejoices in the truth; bears all things, believes all things, hopes all things, endures all things* (1 Corinthians 13:4–7).

Rather than rejoicing in iniquity (sin), in what am I to rejoice?

 **Calling Names**

Let's be specific, girls. Take the movie, *How to Lose a Guy in Ten Days.* "Screenit" tells us that this movie shows repeated drinking, 39 curse words, 9 uses of God's name in vain, and unmarried couples in provocative and passionate sexual situations. What are we thinking? Aren't we "rejoicing in iniquity" (1 Corinthians 13:4–7) when we allow ourselves to be entertained by iniquity?

Let's go back a few years and look at *Titanic.* It seems as if everyone—many Christians included—saw this movie, although reviews tell us that it had 41 curses, 18 uses of our Creator's name in vain, and female nudity! Just because society does it, that does not make it right! God calls us to holy living (1 Peter 1:16). How can we go out and watch these movies on Saturday night and then come in on Sunday morning and sing, "Purer in heart, O God, help me to be"? We have no right to pray, "Do not lead us into temptation" (Matthew 6:13) if we willingly walk into it all the time!

**Music, Books, Magazines, and Radio**

Popular music is another media source laden with immorality. The lyrics contained in many of these songs have profanity, as well as references to drugs, homicide, and suicide. Many songs contain sexually explicit lyrics too. What kinds of role models are these singers, rappers, movie stars, and television personalities?

Unfortunately, television, movies, and music are not the only sources of corrupt media. Many books and magazines contain vulgar articles, scantily dressed models, and perverted ideas. Even magazines directed at teenage girls promote premarital sex and poor body image. In almost every contemporary magazine, there are immodestly dressed models who encourage girls—whether directly or by implication—to look just like them. And we know that teenage girls are already self-conscious about their body images. These stereotypical images certainly do not help.

Morning radio shows often share inappropriate jokes and humor, and radio talk shows are increasingly dirty and biased as well. Everything we have mentioned thus far and things much worse are on the Internet.

**Minds Wasting Away**

Are these types of media suitable for us? Are they best for anyone, for that matter? Do these words and images really affect us negatively? Many studies have reached a definite conclusion on this matter. A recent study has found that almost 75 percent of teenagers say that the portrayal of sex on television influences the sexual behavior of kids their age. The same study also found that 25 percent of teens admit that its portrayal influences their own behavior. Since 49 percent of kids and teenagers do not have parental rules that govern their television watching, teenagers are being exposed to tremendous amounts of immorality through television alone.

A recent study suggests that the average American watches approximately 13.6 hours of television a week and that by the time today's child reaches 70 years old,

Even magazines directed at teenage girls promote premarital sex and poor body image.

## MINDS WASTING AWAY

*Are you spending your time and effort looking into the mirror of culture and trying to be beautiful and successful by the standards of the world, or are you looking into the mirror of the Word, and trying to be what God would have you to be?* (Seeking Spiritual Beauty, p. 7.)

Why should I be accountable for how I spend my time?

he/she will have spent between 7 and 10 years watching television (Knowledge Networks). There are also numerous studies that support evidence that media violence plays a part in shortening one's attention span and decreasing brain activity in the frontal lobe. Also, too much television-watching along with less physical activity leads to childhood obesity and diabetes. Is this healthy for us? Certainly not!

Can our time be spent in better ways? Could we help someone out instead of wasting away our minds? Obviously the devil is hard at work to corrupt us with all this media exposure. We know that Satan walks about "like a roaring lion, seeking whom he may devour" (1 Peter 5:8). We have to make the choice about whether or not to let Satan succeed by deciding what entertainment will fill our own hearts. The Bible tells us that, as Christians, we must have pure hearts (Matthew 5:8). First Timothy 5:22 instructs us to keep ourselves pure, and 2 Timothy 2:22 conveys a similar sentiment. We should not concern ourselves with unimportant worldly matters (Colossians 3:1–2).

**Stop and Think**

Before watching that questionable television show or movie, we must think of our own responsibilities to keep our hearts pure (Proverbs 4:23) and the influence we have on those around us. First Timothy 4:12 tells us that, even though we are young, we must be good examples. In this same manner, we are to "abstain from every form of evil" (1 Thessalonians 5:22). This could apply to many forms of media, such as the music we listen to or the magazines we read.

While we have examined the effect of corrupt media upon us physically and mentally, we must also think about the effects it may have on our spirituality. Oftentimes, the sexual acts or innuendos in movies or television appeal to teenagers' hormones; those words and pictures are there to make us lust! But the Bible tells us to "flee also youthful lusts" (2 Timothy 2:22) and to avoid evil by "denying ungodliness and worldly lusts" (Titus 2:12). We are also forbidden to have fellowship with the "unfruitful works of darkness" (Ephesians 5:11). If this demoralized media is not considered an unfruitful work of darkness, then what is?

**How to Choose**

Not all media is corrupt. As much as it seems that we are completely encompassed by immorality, there are still good books, television shows, and movies out there. Let's consider some questions written by an unknown author to help us make the right choices.

❖ *The Personal Test:* Will doing this make me a better or worse Christian?

❖ *The Social Test:* Will doing it influence others to be better or worse Christians?

❖ *The Practical Test:* Will the results of my doing it be desirable?

❖ *The Universal Test:* If everyone did this, would it improve or degrade society?

If the demoralized media is not considered an unfruitful work of darkness, then what is?

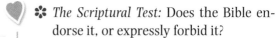

* *The Scriptural Test:* Does the Bible endorse it, or expressly forbid it?

* *The Stewardship Test:* Will my doing this waste the talents God gave me?

* *The Missionary Test:* Will doing this leave me with the proper influence to bring others to Christ?

* *The Character Test:* Will doing this increase my moral and spiritual stamina?

* *The Family Test:* Will doing this bring honor or embarrassment to my family?

* *The Publicity Test:* Would I want other Christians to know about my doing this?

* *The Common Sense Test:* Does doing this agree with plain, everyday common sense?

* *The Financial Test:* Will doing this rob me of my financial ability to do good?

* *The Fairness Test:* If I do this will I be honest and will I be practicing the *Golden Rule?*

## How to Choose

*If then you were raised with Christ, seek those things which are above, where Christ is, sitting at the right hand of God. Set your mind on things above, not on things on the earth* (Colossians 3:1–2).

How does the Bible instruct me to avoid corrupt media? (Give Scripture references.)

In what ways do the media try to misdirect me?

**Oh, Be Careful**

Girls, think seriously. What do you listen to? What do you watch? What do you read? What do you log on to? If we successfully avoid the perverted media, we will become much better Christians. We must evaluate these media sources with a sound mind and good judgment in order to obey God's Word completely. Watching these sorts of television shows and movies, as well as listening to these kinds of music, is

a factor that will help determine our eternal destiny. Do we want to lose our souls over the kind of entertainment we allow into our hearts, or would we rather stay faithful to God and live eternally with Him in heaven?

## Work Cited:

Knowledge Networks. http://knowledgenetworks.com/info/press/releases/2003/100603_kidsbedrooms.htm. "Children's Bedrooms Are Media Havens," October 6, 2003.

Butt, Sheila. *Seeking Spiritual Beauty*. Huntsville, AL: Publishing Designs, Inc., 2002.

# NOTES

# CHAPTER NINE

# Avoiding the Drug Scene

## Hannah Colley and Lora Turner

## Alcoholic Beverages

### Hannah Colley

We've all read the bumper stickers: "Don't drink and drive" and "Friends don't let friends drive drunk." But we rarely hear people say negative things about drinking at times other than when someone is behind the wheel. It is a social activity in which most people participate. So what's the big deal? This chapter will address the issue that most people consider a non-issue.

First, let's take a look at what God has to say about drinking.

❉ "Wine is a mocker, strong drink is a brawler, and whoever is led astray by it is not wise" (Proverbs 20:1).

❉ "Woe to men mighty at drinking wine, woe to men valiant for mixing intoxicating drink, who justify the wicked for a bribe, and take away justice from the righteous man!" (Isaiah 5:22–23).

❉ "For those who sleep, sleep at night, and those who get drunk are drunk at night. But let us who are of the day be sober, putting on the breastplate of

## ALCOHOLIC BEVERAGES

Research: Find your own evidence to prove that drinking alcohol slows mental processing. Look for additional Bible verses on the subject.

*But let us who are of the day be sober, putting on the breastplate of faith and love, and as a helmet the hope of salvation* (1 Thessalonians 5:8).

First Thessalonians 5: 8 instructs "those of us who are of the day." What are those instructions? Are they for me?

faith and love, and as a helmet the hope of salvation" (1 Thessalonians 5:7–8).

❊ "Now the works of the flesh are evident, which are: adultery, fornication, uncleanness, lewdness . . . envy, murders, drunkenness, revelries, and the like; of which I tell you beforehand, just as I also told you in time past, that those who practice such things will not inherit the kingdom of God" (Galatians 5:19–21).

## INTOXICATION

Why do the majority of people think drinking alcohol leads to having fun? When is it *not* fun?

**Intoxication**

The passages above indicate that God vehemently opposes getting drunk. The one that is clearest in my mind is the last one. Galatians 5:19–21 contains a list of actions that will prevent us from entering the kingdom of heaven. Drunkenness is on that list! Did you get that? If unrepented of, one night of such "fun" has eternal consequences.

Besides these obvious reasons not to get drunk, alcohol slows the mind and the body, even after the immediate side effects have subsided. With each drink, brain cells are destroyed, which may slow down thinking and reasoning abilities for the rest of your life. The following statistics give the percentage of students reporting having experienced each of the following potential consequences of drinking during the year prior to completing the Core survey in 2001:

Find a scripture describing the broad vs. the narrow way. Why are most people following the broad way of intoxication?

❊ 64.5 percent had a hangover.

❊ 24.4 percent performed poorly on a test or other project.

❉ 16.5 percent had trouble with police or other authorities.

❉ 31.8 percent got into an argument or fight.

❉ 55.3 percent vomited or became nauseated.

❉ 29.0 percent drove a car while under the influence.

❉ 34.1 percent missed a class.

❉ 34.7 percent suffered memory loss.

❉ 40.5 percent did something they later regretted.

I recently talked with a friend who regretted having become drunk in previous months. He said he never liked the taste of alcohol, but he was pressured to drink it at this certain party. He was a little depressed anyway, so he drank until he was beyond tipsy. He felt awful for at least a week. He did not do well in school, and he felt like a slob. He could not enjoy regular social activities because of that one night of drinking!

My friend's story is very disturbing, but statistics and stories pale in comparison with God's authority. The main thing is that God said drunkenness is wrong and God's will is all that matters. Drunkenness is clearly prohibited by God under any circumstances. That does not mean He does not want us to have fun. He does not say, "I want you to commit social suicide." He says, "I don't want you to get hurt. Please take care of your body, my temple."

God does not say, "I want you to commit social suicide," but, "I don't want you to get hurt."

## MODERATION FALLACY

Why is avoidance of alcoholic beverages the only sure way to avoid drunkenness?

Which is easier?
1) Determining how much alcohol is too much
2) Saying, "I won't participate."

 **Moderation Fallacy**

A teen with big dreams and ambition written all over her face confidently explained her beliefs about drinking to me: "I have come to the decision that to get drunk is an unhealthy choice. With all the statistics about the physical harm of excessive drinking, this might hold me back from my goals. However, I have no problem with drinking occasionally in small amounts." She continued, "I'll still drink beer at parties or whatever, but I'm scared that if I get drunk all the time my talents will suffer."

Think, girls! If each drink destroys brain cells—and it does!—then her logic is flawed. If a lot of alcohol does a lot of harm, then a moderate amount does a moderate amount of harm.

We know from multiple passages of Scripture that God despises drunkenness. What, though, in God's mind, is drunk? Can anyone say for sure? No. God never defined it. He did not limit us to a specific blood-alcohol content level. We cannot know for sure what God meant by *drunk*, so isn't it wise just to avoid alcohol completely?

**My Influence**

Destroyed brain cells are not the only reason to abstain from alcohol. What about your influence? Even if you intend to drink only occasionally and in very small amounts, the people who see you buying or accepting the beverage will assume you participate in and endorse the use of alcoholic beverages. If you want to encourage others—younger people, perhaps—to abstain from drunkenness, you will not be seen purchasing alcoholic beverages. How could you possibly teach others that drunkenness is a sin when they have seen you buying alcohol or perhaps drinking a glass of it? Your unwise action will rob you of that precious opportunity to influence others for good.

A few years ago, I happened upon one of the teenagers from the congregation where we attended. He was hanging out with some other teens in a parking lot. As my family drove by and waved hello, we noticed his passing a beer to the guy sitting beside him. I did not know for sure that he was drinking with them, but if he had ever tried to discourage me from doing it, I would not have been apt to listen after that. Perhaps that seems extreme, but I'm just being honest with you. That's how people react, whether or not they know all the facts. Let's make sure that our influence is the very best it can be in every single setting and situation.

**Decide for Yourself**

I cannot make choices about alcohol for you. You have to decide for yourself. I do want to remind you of something, though. Even if you just drink a little now and then but plan to be through with alcohol by the time you have kids, one day you will regret drinking. Some parents are so afraid when they talk to their kids about drinking and drugs—they fear the question, "Dad (or Mom), did you ever drink?" Don't make choices now that will require you to look your child in the eye one day and say, "Yes, I did." Your ability to keep your children away from alcohol may be

## My Influence

How do I feel when an adult whom I respect exemplifies the attitude: "Don't do as I do; just do as I say"?

Why is my influence so important? Find a scripture to support your answer.

## DECIDE FOR YOURSELF

Imagine standing before God in the Day of Judgment. When I think of my decisions about drinking alcohol, what can motivate me to be serious?

What are my choices regarding alcoholic beverages? Which is the safe choice?

## WHY YOU SHOULD JUST SAY "NO!"

MY REASONS FOR SAYING, "NO!"

❁ _____

_____

❁ _____

_____

forfeited. Children generally feel it is okay to do something their parents have done. That fact has been proved throughout all of time. We even see several biblical examples of children following the footsteps of unwise parents.

Many young people have made mistakes involving alcohol or other choices they now regret. If we have regret over past mistakes hanging over our heads, we need to remember that the redeeming blood of Christ can conquer our guilt! Maybe we will not be able to say to our children, "No, I've never had any alcohol." But instead, we can share a story with them of laying down a sin problem and taking up the cross. No one has made a mistake that Christ cannot forgive and help her to overcome. Even starting today, you can work to build a constantly purer life.

If we have never been partakers of alcoholic beverages, we will be wise in continuing to choose to abstain from all forms of drinking. God will bless us for it!

**If Only**

One final thought: Alcoholism is, by all standards, a major problem in our society. But think about this: If everyone in America agreed with the points I have made about completely avoiding alcohol, the problem would not exist. No drunken-driver accidents. No accidental overdoses. No hungry children whose livelihood is spent on alcoholic beverages. Consider the following:

❁ *Those who refuse to experiment with alcohol never become alcoholics.* Even those with genetic predispositions to alcoholism will not become alcoholics if they avoid the first drink.

❉ *Many alcoholics never intended to become such when they took their first drinks. Why take the chance?*

**One Safe Choice**

There are several choices regarding alcohol use: total abstinence, social drinking, private drinking, and excessive drinking. There is only one safe choice for Christians: Abstain!

# Why You Should Just Say No!

*Lora Turner*

Most of us have attended a school with a drug program in its curriculum. Since before we can remember, teachers and parents have told us, "Just say no!" But somewhere between being a young child who comes home with "Be All You Can Be: Stay Drug Free" stickers or D. A. R. E. T-shirts and becoming a young adult, we have to make a deliberate choice about how to live and how to treat our bodies. What are the facts?

❉ Among 12- to 17-year-olds, use of drugs—including cocaine and hallucinogens—increased from 8.2 percent in 1994 to 10.9 percent in 1995 (National Household Survey on Drug Abuse [NHSDA]).

## TRUE CONFESSIONS OF AN ADDICT

*I've been a heroin addict for 12 years. I started drinking when I was 14 years old. Then I started smoking weed. I did a little acid in high school. Things really started to accelerate when I got to college. I started tripping on mushrooms every chance I got. Then I moved on to LSD every weekend. In 1990 I graduated and immediately someone said, "Try some of this; it's Blues powder." That's when I started sniffing heroin. I knew immediately that it was stronger than me, but I was clueless. I also started freebasing. I would stop and start over and over again. Back then kicking cold turkey was an easy three-day kick, five tops. After about five years of sniffing I wanted to see what shooting was all about. Once this began it was near impossible to stop. I got bored with the heroin and someone turned me on to speedballs. That was it for me. My habit went through the roof, two bundles of dope to buffer the three grams of coke a day, I was a dealer. From then on I've been in and out of institutions, 12 detox centers, two rehabs and a methadone clinic in four years, but during my last run which lasted two and a half years I was unable to get more than a three day stay in a detox because of insurance. My hardest kick was 17 days and not a wink of sleep. They wouldn't even give me a sleeping pill. Every time I asked for some kind of relief they would tell me to go away and stop fooling around.*

❖ Marijuana use increased among young people 12-17 from 6 percent in 1994 to 8.2 percent in 1995 (NHSDA).

❖ Marijuana use by eighth-graders has increased every year since 1991 (Monitoring the Future, a national survey of 8th-, 10th-, and 12th-graders.)

Let's consider some principles from the Bible that will help us make the right choices:

❖ *Drugs hinder a Christian's ability to be sober and make good decisions* (Titus 2:12). In Titus 2 (KJV), God calls on Christians to deny ungodliness and live soberly in this world. *Sober* comes from the Greek word *sophronos*, which describes someone who is temperate, quiet and sedate in demeanor, serious, showing self-control, and has a sound mind. Do any of these characteristics describe someone on drugs? Certainly not. It is of utmost importance that you keep a sound mind so you can make intelligent choices between right and wrong.

In Leviticus 10, God told the Old Testament priests not to drink wine or intoxicating drink so "you may distinguish between holy and unholy, and between unclean and clean, and that you may teach . . . all the statutes which the Lord has spoken" (Leviticus 10:9–11). God knows that certain substances affect our minds and interfere with proper judgment. Christians—we all serve as God's priests today (1 Peter 2:9)—still have the responsibility of maintaining clear minds and pure

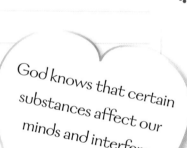

God knows that certain substances affect our minds and interfere with proper judgment.

bodies as to distinguish between holy and unholy living. Otherwise, how can Christians shine as lights in a dark world? (Philippians 2:15).

❋ *Drug use hurts others* (Philippians 2:4). Every decision you make affects the people around you. Every destructive decision you make negatively affects those around you. Let's look at some Bible examples. Consider Lot's choice to live among sinners and how that choice affected his family (Genesis 19), how Pharaoh's hardened heart hurt his entire country (Exodus 12), and how Achan's greed destroyed his family (Joshua 7).

Any destructive choice you make will hurt not only yourself, but others as well. I know a Christian brother who has chosen a life of drugs. His family's reputation is ruined. His loved ones spend most of their nights worried about where he is and what he is doing. He wastes the family's money on drugs. He has even resorted to stealing to fund his habit and has been in jail several times. His family will never be the same. Drug use tears families apart, destroying relationships that are essential in a growing Christian's life.

❋ *We will be held accountable before God for how we use our bodies.* Drugs destroy God's temple (1 Corinthians 6:19; 2 Corinthians 5:10). We sing a devotional song called "I Am Mine No More." This song describes exactly the way we should think of all our possessions: "I've been bought with blood,

## DRUGS HINDER A CHRISTIAN'S ABILITY TO BE SOBER AND MAKE GOOD DECISIONS

What Scriptures tell me that God knows that certain substances can affect my mind and interfere with proper judgment?

How can I possibly be hurt if one in my family chooses to use drugs?

When a girl is baptized into Christ, she surrenders everything to God, including her body.

## NICOTINE

Nicotine is as addictive as heroin or cocaine, which makes it extremely difficult to quit. Those who start smoking before the age of 21 have the hardest time breaking the habit.

How are teens encouraged to use nicotine?

and I am mine no more." When a person is baptized into Christ, she surrenders everything to God, including her body. She becomes a steward over what God has given her. Her body belongs to God, so she must choose to use it in a way that pleases Him. Paul asked in 1 Corinthians 6:19: "Do you not know that your body is the temple of the Holy Spirit . . . and you are not your own?" In the Old Testament, God dwelled in a physical temple, but Christians today harbor Christ in their hearts. Our bodies are the dwelling place of God on earth and should be "a vessel for honor, sanctified and useful for the Master" (2 Timothy 2:21). Look at the effects of some of the more popular drugs on the body (Encyclopedia Britannica Online):

1. Nicotine: Nicotine is a powerful and addictive stimulant found in most tobacco products. It is one of 40 carcinogens (cancer-causing substances) found in cigarettes. Nicotine is typically smoked in cigarettes or cigars. Some people put a pinch of tobacco (called chewing or smokeless tobacco) into their mouths and absorb nicotine through the lining of their mouths.

   Effects and Dangers: Rapid heartbeat, increased blood pressure, shortness of breath, greater likelihood of colds and flu, emphysema, chronic bronchitis, stomach ulcers, weakened immunity.

2. Marijuana (pot, weed, blunts, chronic, grass, reefer, herb, ganja): Marijuana is the most commonly used illegal drug in the United States. It is typically smoked in cigarettes (joints), hollowed-out cigars (blunts), pipes (bowls), or water pipes (bongs). Some people mix it with foods or brew it as a tea. Marijuana is a gateway drug. Its use often leads to the use of more potent illegal drugs.

> Effects & Dangers: Alters mood and coordination. Causes mood swings that range from stimulated or happy to drowsy or depressed. Accelerates heart rate and blood pressure. Causes red eyes, drowsiness, and hunger; dry mouth and throat, lack of coordination, decreased blood sugar and body temperature, lung damage, decreased fertility, weakened immunity, stunted growth, depression, paranoia, and hallucination.

3. Cocaine and crack (coke, snow, blow, nose candy, white, big C stardust, freebase, rock): Cocaine is a white crystalline powder made from the dried leaves of the coca plant. Crack—it crackles when heated—is made from cocaine. It looks like white or tan pellets. Cocaine is inhaled through the nose or injected. Crack is smoked. Cocaine addicts many people after their first try.

> Effects and Dangers: Rocks the central nervous system, giving users a quick, intense feeling of power and energy. (Snorting highs last between 15 and

## MARIJUANA

Teens who use marijuana can become psychologically dependent upon it. In addition, their bodies may demand more and more marijuana to achieve the same kind of high experienced in the beginning.

## WHAT'S LIFE LIKE ON DRUGS?

Drug Awareness Resistance Education (DARE) ambassadors (high school students working with elementary and middle school drug prevention programs) asked tough questions of five recovering drug addicts in Kansas City, Kansas:

*The first time was great. The depressing part is I never duplicated that first time. I kept trying. Sports and physical fitness had been biggies in my life, but I went the complete opposite way after that first hit. I lived two lives, had two sets of friends. I didn't care what happened in the process; I wanted to reproduce that first effect. It got depressing never finding it. Appearing to be in a coma became the next best thing. It became a game going through life with only my heart and lungs working. While I was in that stage, nothing could have gotten me off—not coaches I once idealized—no one! I know now, I'll never be a "social drug user," never be able to drink a beer with the guys and then go home.*

## COCAINE AND CRACK

Cocaine and crack are highly addictive, and as a result, the drug, not the user, calls the shots. (Snorting can also put a hole inside the lining of your nose.) Using either of these drugs even one time can kill you.

## HEROIN

Heroin creates a need for more as soon as possible just to feel good again. Withdrawal is intense and symptoms include insomnia, vomiting, and muscle pain.

## METHAMPHETAMINES

Methamphetamine users feel a euphoric rush, particularly if it is smoked or shot up. But they can develop tolerance quickly—and will use more meth for longer periods of time, resulting in sleeplessness, paranoia, and hallucinations. Violent, aggressive behavior, psychosis, and brain damage are consequences of long-term use.

30 minutes; smoking highs last between 5 and 10 minutes.) Elevates vital signs. Causes insomnia, chronic fatigue, anxiety, paranoia, hallucinations, lung damage, and convulsions. May cause hepatitis or AIDS for those who share needles.

4. Heroin (horse, smack, Big H, junk): Heroin comes from the dried milk of the opium poppy, which is also used to create the class of painkillers called narcotics—medicines such as codeine and morphine. Heroin can range from a white to dark brown powder to a sticky, tar-like substance. It is very dangerous because it is mostly injected directly into the bloodstream, but can be smoked or inhaled (if it is pure).

Heroin is extremely addictive and easy to overdose on, which can cause death. Withdrawal is intense and symptoms include insomnia, vomiting, and muscle pain.

Effects and Dangers: Gives a burst of euphoric (high) feelings, especially if it's injected. (This high is often followed by drowsiness, nausea, stomach cramps, and vomiting.) Causes chronic constipation, dry skin, scarred veins, breathing problems, nausea, slowed breathing, cold, moist and discolored skin, convulsions, and coma.

5. Methamphetamines (speed, meth, crank, crystal, chalk, fire, glass, crypto, ice): Methamphetamine, also called "crystal meth" depending on its form, is a designer drug. This means that drug chemists create it

by slightly altering an already existing drug, amphetamine, to stay ahead of drug laws. It can be swallowed, snorted, injected, or smoked.

Effects and Dangers: Causes intense delusions such as believing that there are insects crawling under the skin. Causes dry mouth, nervousness, headaches, blurred vision, sweating, moodiness, malnutrition, skin disorders, ulcers, heart tremors, stroke, or paralysis.

6. LSD (acid, blotter, doses, microdots): LSD (which stands for lysergic acid diethylamide) is a lab-brewed hallucinogen and mood-changing chemical. Odorless, colorless, and tasteless, LSD is licked or sucked off small squares of blotting paper. Capsules and liquid forms are swallowed. Paper squares containing acid may be decorated with cute cartoon characters or colorful designs.

Effects and Dangers: Induces panic attacks, confusion, depression, and frightening delusions. Causes sleeplessness, mangled speech, convulsions, increased heart rate, and coma; strong mood swings, perspiration, chills, and decreased appetite.

7. Ecstasy (XTC, X, Adam, E, Roll): This is the fastest growing designer drug created by underground chemists. It comes in powder, tablet, or capsule form. Ecstasy is a popular club drug among teens because it is widely available at raves, dance clubs, and

## AN AFFAIR WITH DRUGS

*My affair with drugs started when I was a 17-year-old student. I had a reputation as a real party girl, who was up for anything. My boyfriend was a DJ and drugs were always readily available on the music scene. When you're young, you just think you're invincible. I carried on partying throughout my early twenties, even when we had our son. But then two years ago, I walked out on them both. I just couldn't cope with the responsibility of being a parent and I lost custody of my son. That was the start of my depression. Most of my friends had now started to settle down but I was living my twenties in reverse. I had a job in the city with loads of disposable cash and I started hanging out with similar people. I couldn't handle going home alone, so I'd just stay out as late as possible. My weekend would start on Thursday afternoon and between then and Sunday night, I'd use four to six grams of coke. I was also drinking a lot, sleeping around, and losing loads of weight.*

## LSD

Hallucinations occur within 30 to 90 minutes of dropping acid. Users see colors or hear sounds with other delusions such as melting walls and a loss of any sense of time.

concerts. Ecstasy is swallowed or sometimes snorted.

Effects and Dangers: Causes a tingly skin sensation, dry mouth, cramps, blurred vision, chills, sweating, nausea, hallucinations, vomiting, and convulsions. Users may chew on something—like a pacifier—to relieve the symptom of jaw clenching.

## ECSTASY

Ecstasy combines a hallucinogenic and a stimulant effect, intensifying emotions. It sends the teen body into overdrive, allowing one to dance for hours into the night. Long-term, it damages memory and motor function. Depression, anxiety, and confusion often occur. Hyperthermia (fevers of over 105 degrees) and dehydration cause deaths linked to ecstasy.

## ROHYPNOL

Even though a depressant, Rohypnol causes some people to be overly excited or aggressive. It is associated with date rape. Many teen girls and women have reported rape after Rohypnol was slipped into their drinks.

## INHALANTS

Inhalants make you feel giddy and confused, as if you were drunk. They are the most likely of abused substances to cause severe toxic reaction and death. Using inhalants, even one time, can kill you.

8. Rohypnol (pronounced: ro-hip'-nol) (roofies, roach, forget-me pill, date rape drug): A low-cost, increasingly popular drug, rohypnol often comes in presealed bubble packs, so many teens think the drug is safe. This drug is swallowed, sometimes with alcohol or other drugs. Rohypnol is a prescription anti-anxiety medication that is ten times more powerful than Valium.

Effects and Dangers: Memory loss, drowsiness, dizziness, upset stomach. The drug also causes "anterograde amnesia." (This means it's hard to remember what happened while on the drug, like a blackout. Because of this it can be hard to give important details if a young woman wants to report a rape.)

9. Inhalants: Inhalants are substances that are sniffed or "huffed" to give the user an immediate rush or high. They include household products like glues, paint thinners, dry cleaning fluids, gasoline, felt-tip marker fluid, correction fluid, hair spray, aerosol deodorants, and spray paint. Inhalants are breathed in directly from the original container (sniffing

or snorting), from a plastic bag (bagging), or by holding an inhalant-soaked rag in the mouth (huffing).

Effects and Dangers: Users get headaches and nosebleeds. They may also lose their sense of hearing and sense of smell. Huffing, snorting, or bagging even once can be fatal.

You will give account for the way you use God's temple. "For we must all appear before the judgment seat of Christ, that each one may receive the things done in the body . . . whether good or bad" (2 Corinthians 5:10). Where do you want to stand on judgment day?

**The Sure Cure**

Will drugs solve your problems? Will they make you happy? Some teens believe drugs will help them think better or be more popular. Others are simply curious: "One try won't hurt!" Others want to fit in. A few use drugs to gain attention from their parents. Others use drugs because they are depressed or think drugs will help them escape their problems. The truth is, drugs don't solve problems. Drugs simply hide feelings and problems. When a drug wears off, the feelings and problems remain—or become worse. Drugs can ruin every aspect of a person's life.

Christ gives us a sense of completeness that cannot be found with drugs (Romans 15:13). It has been theorized that we all have a "God-shaped hole" in our life, a space that only God can fill. And until becoming a Christian, each of us searches for something to fill that hole. Some try to

# WHAT CAN I DO TO FEEL GOOD WITHOUT DRUGS?

1) Exercise. (Working out, walking/hiking/admiring nature). "I feel good after I do those things."

2) Help others. "I volunteered at an animal shelter a few years ago, and helping others in need (people or animals) is a natural high. It really is."

3) Play games. "Playing a card game or a board game makes me feel great."

Browse through the previous pages and note which drugs can kill the user after just one time.

Go back and underline the drugs that you had never heard of before this study.

## THE SURE CURE

*Let us hear the conclusion of the whole matter: Fear God and keep His commandments, for this is man's all (Ecclesiastes 12:13).*

*Now may the God of hope fill you with all joy and peace in believing, that you may abound in hope by the power of the Holy Spirit (Romans 15:13).*

What verse in Ecclesiastes verifies the fact that I have a "God-shaped hole" in my life that only He can fill?

fill it with money. Some try to fill it with an earthly relationship. Some try to fill it with drugs. Take Solomon, for example. He tried to fill the space in his life with every earthly pleasure and luxury. His conclusion? Vanity! All is vanity! Solomon found the answer: Only God and our obedience to Him give us the fullness we need in our lives (Ecclesiastes 12:13).

Romans 15:13 teaches that God can fill you with all joy and peace in believing, that you may abound in hope. Christians have the hope of living in paradise forever with God. Why would you want to ruin your life with drugs when you have so much to hope for?

If you have a problem, don't use drugs to escape it. Get help from a Christian counselor. Pray. "In everything . . . let your requests be made known to God; and the peace of God, which surpasses all understanding, will guard your hearts" (Philippians 4:6–7). The only way to have true peace and contentment and joy in your life is through Christ, not through drugs.

## Additional Sources:

For more information on drugs and overcoming drug problems, contact one of these services: National Clearinghouse for Alcohol and Drug Information (1-800-729-6686) or Higher Education Center for Alcohol and Other Drug Prevention (1-800-676-1730).

## Works Cited:

"2001 Statistics on Alcohol and other Drug Use."

htpp://www.siu.edu/departments/corenist/public_html/recent.html, Core Institute, 2001.

"2005 Drugs, What You Should Know"

http://kidshealth.org/teen/drug_alcohol/drugs/know_about_drugs.html.

"Cocaine." Encyclopedia Britannica. 2004. Encyclopedia Britannica Online. 2 March 2004. <http://search.eb.com/eb/article?eu=24947>.

"Marijuana." Encyclopedia Britannica. 2004. Encyclopedia Britannica Online. 2 March 2004. <http://search.eb.com/eb/article?eu=52181>.

"Nicotine." Encyclopedia Britannica. 2004. Encyclopedia Britannica Online. 2 March 2004. <http://search.eb.com/eb/article?eu=57163>.

Brennan, Kristine. *Junior Drug Awareness: Ecstasy and Other Designer Drugs.* Philadelphia: Chelsea House Publishers, 2000.

De Angelis, Gina. *Junior Drug Awareness: Nicotine and Cigarettes.* Philadelphia: Chelsea House Publishers, 2000.

Friedman, David. *Focus on Drugs and the Brain.* Philadelphia: 21st Century Books, 1990.

Peacock, Nancy B. *Junior Drug Awareness: Alcohol.* Philadelphia: Chelsea House Publishers, 2000.

Rogak, Lisa. *Steroids: Dangerous Game.* Minneapolis: Lerner Publications Company, 1992.

Shulman, Jeffrey. *The Drug-Alert Dictionary and Resource Guide.* Frederick, MD: 21st Century Books, 1991.

Spence, Annette. *Encyclopedia of Good Health: Substance Abuse.* Facts on New York: File Publishing, 1989.

Whitaker, Anita. *Straddling the Fence: The Danger of Compromise.* Huntsville, AL: Publishing Designs, Inc., 2002.

## More Hotlines:

National Institute on Drug Abuse
1-800-662-4357

National Cocaine Hotline
1-800-262-2463

National Council on Alcoholism and Drug Dependency Hotline
1-800-622-2255

Just Say No International
1-800-258-2766

National Association of Alcoholism and Drug Abuse Counselors
1-800-548-0497

## Recommended Reading:

Duke, Kerry. *God at a Distance.* Huntsville, AL: Publishing Designs, Inc., 1995.

Whitaker, Anita. *Straddling the Fence.* Huntsville, AL: Publishing Designs, Inc., 2002.

CHAPTER TEN

# Talking the Talk

### Hannah Colley

One of the most powerful tools women use is verbal communication. Are you aware that women speak from 30 to 50 percent more words each day than men do? That means that as girls we can do 30 to 50 percent more good or 30 to 50 percent more evil than our male counterparts. Just think about that!

What you are inside comes out when you talk. People judge you by the words you say (Matthew 12:34; Luke 6:45). Choosing the right words for each conversation is a vital task. This chapter will include some practical ways we as Christian girls can speak to please God. Remember these four "d" questions as you strive to use your words as a means of edification rather than destruction:

❁ Is it dirty?

❁ Is it disrespectful?

❁ Is it destructive?

❁ Is it deceptive?

## Is It Dirty?

> For our exhortation did not come from error or uncleanness, nor was it in deceit. But as we have been approved by God to be entrusted with the gospel, even so we

## TALKING THE TALK

*Finally, brethren, whatever things are true, whatever things are noble, whatever things are just, whatever things are pure, whatever things are lovely, whatever things are of good report, if there is any virtue and if there is anything praiseworthy—meditate on these things* (Philippians 4:8).

*But those things which proceed out of the mouth come from the heart, and they defile a man* (Matthew 15:18).

Read the two previous verses. How can you tie the meanings together?

_____

_____

How do our thoughts relate to our speech?

_____

_____

speak, not as pleasing men, but God who tests our hearts (1 Thessalonians 2:3–4).

I looked up the word *unclean*—"dirty" as we would say—in *Thayer's Greek-English Lexicon of the New Testament.* The first definition was in reference to our bodies being dirty; but notice the second definition: "In a moral sense, the impurity of lustful, luxurious, profligate living." According to Paul in this verse, the words people speak can reflect a "lustful, luxurious, profligate" lifestyle.

When writing this chapter, I struggled with the decision of whether or not I should travel, word by word, through the enormous world of foul language. I decided that most girls reading this book already know just about every repugnant word our peers use, whether they learned them at school, at play rehearsal, or perhaps even among your youth group—I hope not! Many words which conjure up impure sexual visions in our minds are frequently thrown around in our world like leaves on a windy day.

We can hardly escape hearing vulgarities about various parts of the body, about sexuality, or about obscene subjects. You know. You hear these words. There are many words that are recognized as dirty words, but there are also some that are considered mild in our culture.

Even though I said I would not define specific words, there is one phrase that seems to fool everyone, even Christians. We all hear constantly, and you might use it without any tinge of guilt: "this or that sucks." Before you start rolling your eyes

> We can hardly escape hearing vulgarities about various parts of the body or obscene subjects.

116

and calling me radical, please read what it means. The definition of the word *sucks* used as a slang term means "engages in fellatio (oral sex)." As I am writing this, I am blushing with embarrassment, but I feel that you should know the true meaning of this word which has become so socially acceptable.

I certainly cannot see the logic behind a Christian's using this phrase after reading Philippians 4:8:

> Finally, brethren, whatever things are true, whatever things are noble, whatever things are just, whatever things are pure, whatever things are lovely, whatever things are of good report, if there is any virtue and if there is anything praiseworthy—meditate on these things.

Does such a phrase fit into any of those categories? The answer is obvious.

Not only do I want to encourage you to keep your mouth clean of foul language, but I also pray that God will give you enough courage to say something when you hear those around you use such speech. If you are in doubt about the meaning of a slang word, look it up. Stand up for what you believe. Chances are, your friends will respect you for it. Practice asking politely that they not use those words in your presence. When my friends ask me why, I simply tell them that hearing them use such language makes it difficult for me to keep my own words and thoughts pure. If you are kind and gentle in your request, they will probably make the effort to accommodate your wishes. If not, they do not respect you, and they are probably not the type of people you need to hang around.

## Is It Dirty?

Read the following verse and then write it in your own words.

*For every tree is known by its own fruit. For men do not gather figs from thorns, nor do they gather grapes from a bramble bush. A good man out of the good treasure of his heart brings forth good; and an evil man out of the evil treasure of his heart brings forth evil. For out of the abundance of the heart his mouth speaks. But why do you call Me "Lord, Lord" and do not do the things which I say? (Luke 6:44–46).*

117

## 💜 Is It Disrespectful?

Many words and phrases that blaspheme my Lord have become commonplace. Most people just do not think about the meaning of these words.

When your friends say, "Oh my God," they probably are not talking about God at all. They are using His holy name merely as an interjection, an expression of surprise or shock. You may hear, "Oh my gosh," "Lord, yes," or "Lord, no," "Jeez," "Golly," or "Gee." All of these are euphemisms for the Lord's name. They are not used to reverence God. A euphemism is a substitute for a word that we all recognize to be truly offensive.

Even the law of Moses forbade the improper use of God's name:

> You shall not take the name of the Lord your God in vain, for the Lord will not hold him guiltless who takes His name in vain (Exodus 20:7).

That means they could not use His name lightly, but only with reverence. One chilling thought indicated in the words, "the Lord will not hold him guiltless," is that when they used His name vainly, they were guilty before God.

The New Testament reminds us that Christians also are held accountable for our use of God's name. Hebrews 12:28 teaches us to "serve God acceptably with reverence and fear." Paul was chosen to bear His name "before Gentiles, kings, and the children of Israel" (Acts 9:15). Jesus taught His disciples to pray: "Hallowed be Your name."

> The New Testament reminds us that Christians are held accountable for our use of God's name.

Other words we call curse words are more easily recognized. *Darn* and *dang* are euphemisms for *damn*.

*Hell* is often used lightly, as well. *Heck* is a softer version of *hell*.

Let us be sure that the words we use are reflecting the respect we have toward our Creator.

**Is It Destructive?**

Studies have shown that a boy tends to release anger or jealousy by some physical act, like giving their enemies a knuckle sandwich, while a girl's greatest weapon is her tongue. For example, if Bill stole Jim's girlfriend, Jim might walk up to Bill and punch him in the nose. Let's look at a different scenario, this time using girls.

> Pam has had a crush on Henry since sixth grade. Henry never asked her out, but she always knew he was attracted to her. They passed notes in class and sat together during lunch. Then Jan—pretty Jan!—moved to town. Within one week, Henry had asked Jan out on a date. Instead of walking up to Jan and slapping her, Pam began talking about Jan to all her classmates, making up stories that put Jan in a negative light and embellishing true stories to make Jan look bad.

You know what I'm talking about. We girls use words as tools to push someone else down while elevating ourselves. Before you say something about someone else, be sure you ask yourself why you want to say it. Will saying this help the person you're talking about or will it hurt that person? Always consider whether or not you would want the same things said about you. If

## Is It Disrespectful?

How does hearing others using God's name carelessly make it more difficult for me to reverence God?

*Do not be rash with your mouth, and let not your heart utter anything hastily before God. For God is in heaven and you on earth; therefore let your words be few* (Ecclesiastes 5:2).

What foolish actions might I commit when I forget God does not hear my words?

Look up Acts 17:27–28. How do I know God is near?

## Is It Destructive?

What is gossip? Write your definition here:

Think of an example when even my tone of voice may start gossip.

## Is It Destructive?

Note to teacher or class leader:
The following verses are from
the New King James Version.
Have a class member bring a
New American Bible to class.
Ask her to give a two-minute
report on the meaning of
Romans 1:28–32. Have her
compare the phrases "they are
whisperers" and "approve of
those who practice them" to
their equivalent phrases in the
New American Standard Bible.

*And even as they did not like
to retain God in their knowledge,
God gave them over to a debased
mind, to do those things which
are not fitting; being filled with
all unrighteousness, sexual
immorality, wickedness, covetousness, maliciousness; full of envy,
murder, strife, deceit, evil-
mindedness; they are whisperers,
backbiters, haters of God, violent,
proud, boasters, inventors of evil
things, disobedient to parents,
undiscerning, untrustworthy,
unloving, unforgiving, unmerciful;
who, knowing the righteous
judgment of God, that those who
practice such things are deserving
of death, not only do the same
but also approve of those
who practice them (Romans
1:28–32, emphasis added).*

not, then don't say it! (Matthew 7:12).
That applies to what you listen to, as well.
If your friends are trash-talking someone
you know, ask them to stop or simply leave
the room. Rather than breaking others
down with your tongue, use your tongue
to build others up by your kindness. Strike
up a conversation with someone who is
sitting alone. Don't let yourself be a part
of some exclusive clique. Don't let anyone
feel unwanted or out of place. New studies show that the part of your brain that
registers pain reacts the same way when
you feel socially rejected as when you have
been poked in the eye. In other words, it
hurts to be an outcast!

Don't gossip. It hurts others and will
eventually hurt you. Include everyone in
conversations and treat everyone with
kindness. I know that is hard, especially
if there is someone you "just can't stand."
God tells us in Romans 12:20–21:

Therefore "If your enemy is hungry, feed
him; if he is thirsty, give him a drink; for
in so doing you will heap coals of fire on
his head." Do not be overcome by evil, but
overcome evil with good.

If you really want to get back, show
your enemy kindness. She probably will
not quite know how to respond. She might
respond with returned kindness. Let God
handle the vengeance.

Compliments are vital in the life of a
teenage girl. Use your tongue to compliment others about something they said,
their performance in a ballgame or a play,
or simply their appearance. Some people
will respect you instantly if you just en-

courage them with your words. Younger girls especially respond to compliments. I remember the thrill I experienced as a little girl when a teenager said something nice to me. I thought about her compliment for days. Younger girls want to be just like you. Show them the kindness of a Christian. Occasionally send them little notes of encouragement or ask them to sit with you in worship. Little girls sometimes look to teenage girls as their role models more than they do their own parents, whether the parents like it or not. We must take on that grave responsibility and be someone who is okay to emulate.

Avoid making curt remarks:

❉ "She thinks she's all that!"

❉ "Look at those shoes. They must be her mother's."

❉ "She's such a flirt!"

❉ "I think Fran forgot to rinse her hair after washing it this morning."

❉ "She's the only one that just doesn't get it."

❉ "Does it look like I care?"

Learn to encourage with your words:

❉ "She impresses me. She's got spunk!"

❉ "I'm really proud of the way you stood up for what was right."

❉ "I'm here for you if you need me."

❉ "I just want you to know that I'm praying for you."

❉ "You really encourage me!"

## DON'T GOSSIP

*And besides they learn to be idle, wandering about from house to house, and not only idle but also gossips and busybodies, saying things which they ought not* (1 Timothy 5:13).

How does being idle lead to gossip?

When a gossiper repents of her sin, how can I help her to use her time more constructively?

Find a verse in Scripture about being kind. Why is this command often neglected?

Think of words used in trash-talk. How do they contrast with encouraging and complimentary words?

What are some lies that have been told about me?

How did they make me feel?

Who is the father of all lies?

### Is It Deceptive?

Speech that deceives is also condemned in Scripture. The Bible is clear when it comes to lying. In Revelation 21:8 God says, "All liars shall have their part in the lake which burns with fire and brimstone, which is the second death."

There are lots of ways we may deceive with our words. Here are a few.

❋ *An outright lie—the obvious lie.* If your little sister got ketchup all over your history report and, upon your asking, said that she did not do it, that is an outright lie.

❋ *A "technical" truth.* Have you ever said, "Well, technically I was telling the truth"? As an example, let's say you answer the phone, and the person on the line says he wants to talk to your sister. You know it's someone your sister does not want to talk to, so you do your sister a favor—push her out the back door and reply, "Sorry, she's out." Technically, that's the truth, but the deceit, the essence of what you said, is a lie.

❋ *False flattery.* Even if you mean well, lying to make someone else feel good is wrong. Perhaps you have a good friend who did not like the way she looked, so she dyed her black hair blonde and got a perm, and it looks so bad. You know she has low self-esteem as it is, so when she asks, you just say, "Yeah, it looks cool!" You know it would hurt her feelings if you tell her what you really think, so you just tell a little lie. That would be false flattery.

It would hurt her feelings to tell her what you really think, so you just tell a little lie.

❋ *Assent to someone else's lie.* Imagine that you go spend the evening with your best friend, even though you both have to take the ACT the next morning. Before coming to pick you up, your friend told her mom that the two of you were going to study together, so her mom said okay. Instead of studying, you meet your boyfriends at the movies. When you get back to your friend's house to spend the night, your friend's mom says, "Did you go to the library to study?" Your friend says, "Yeah." Then her mom looks at you and says, "Did you have fun?" to which you reply, "Yeah, I did." You had fun, but not doing what your friend said you did.

We have all heard that a lie just gets bigger and bigger because when we tell one, we have to tell another to cover for the first one. There is no form of lying which is okay. Little white lies will condemn us just the same as big black lies. I would much rather face the consequences of telling the truth now than to suffer later eternal consequences for lying.

**Keep Speech Pure**

If you see yourself in any of the above examples, I pray that you will seek the bountiful forgiveness that God is willing to give us, and the forgiveness of those to whom or about whom you have spoken wrongly.

## IS IT DECEPTIVE?

### WAYS TO DECEIVE

❋ An outright lie
❋ A "technical" truth
❋ False flattery
❋ Assent to someone else's lie

What deceit was practiced by Rebekah in the Old Testament? Observe your friends or classmates in the coming week—what kinds of deceit do you notice?

> Face the consequences of telling the truth now, rather than suffer later eternal consequences for lying.

❀ Is it dirty?

❀ Is it disrespectful?

❀ Is it destructive?

❀ Is it deceptive?

May we all remember to ask these four "d" questions as we strive to keep our speech pure, and to the glory of our heavenly Father.

# CHAPTER ELEVEN

# Dating and Waiting

### Lyndsay Pierce and Allison Boyd

## Where, Oh Where, Is Mr. Right?

**Lyndsay Pierce**

It's almost midnight, and Kourtney runs into her house. She says, "Hey Mom! . . . Yeah? . . . Oh, I had a great time!" Then, she runs up the stairs and into her room where she shuts the door and gets out her cell phone. "Hey! . . . Melissa? . . . Yeah, it was such an awesome date . . . Well, first we went to dinner. And then you know we went to see the movie . . . What? . . . Oh, did he touch me? Well, yeah, I mean the movie *was* two hours long! So, I didn't really see all of it, but I sure enjoyed being with him." Kourtney can tell from the silence that Melissa isn't quite sure about all that, so she adds, "Oh, come on Melissa, you're so nit-picky! You know it was all fine. Besides, we really love each other. He told me so for the first time tonight and we'll probably get married anyway when we finish high school."

When it comes to dating, the world sort of has the idea that "anything goes." The world will tell us that as long as we love someone (or think we do!) then, whatever we want to do is okay. We should make

> "What? Oh, did he touch me? Well, yeah. Oh, come on, Melissa, you're so nit-picky!"

## WHERE, OH WHERE, IS MR. RIGHT?

Contrast the world's morality with the Bible's morality.

What are my challenges regarding waiting for a serious relationship?

> Paula was kidding around with her friend Stacey.
> "Yeah, you like Matt sooo much! But he talks dirty—he doesn't even pretend to be a Christian. And you just can't wait to go out with him again!"
> "Oh, give me a break, Paula," quipped Stacey. "It's just a date; I'm not going to marry him!"

How many times have you heard that someone got married before she had "just a date"?

How much emphasis should I place on qualifications for the guys I date?

sure that everything we do is done in love, but the Bible teaches us about a love that is so much higher and exciting than what many in the world mistake as love. It isn't love that motivates us to harm other people with lust or disrespect.

Obviously, the world's philosophy on dating does not fit in with God's plan for Christian dating. God has a plan for Christian women to marry and bring up children in the knowledge of the Lord, but before marriage comes a process of learning about yourself and men and the compatibility between you and a man. Yes, this process may seem long and weary while waiting for Mr. Right to come along, but dating is a significant part in finding your future husband.

This chapter will discuss different aspects and stages of dating. We need to remember that what may be best for us at one stage in our lives could be very harmful to us at another time. For example, just being practical will tell us that our early teen years and time in middle school is probably not the time when we're going to find a husband. But it is a perfect time for growing spiritually, making great guy friends, establishing standards, and becoming aware of what you expect out of yourself and others!

Also, many of us are not going to be ready to commit to a lasting love in marriage right after high school. It may be best for us to get to know different guys in high school rather than to get involved in serious relationships that tempt us to give too much physically or emotionally.

So as you read this chapter, consider where you are in life, pray, talk to your parents, and make choices that are best, practical, and spiritually helpful to you!

**Tips for Preteens and Young Teens**

There is no reason to rush into dating! Waiting to date has several advantages. First, the longer a girl waits, the more time she has to develop her own personality and standards. She can have an understanding of her own expectations and avoid saying yes to just anyone who asks. Also, as girls wait longer, they can form valuable friendships with a large group of people, develop their own interests, and avoid the temptation to practice impurity at a time when hormones run high. Waiting will make the first dates more meaningful and will increase a girl's appreciation for great Christian guys.

Here are some practical suggestions for preserving your purity and making wise choices in dating:

❉ Have godly friends and only accept dates with godly guys (Psalm 119:63; Ecclesiastes 4:9–12).

❉ Avoid tempting situations: alone, dark, with other couples who show too much affection (1 Corinthians 6:18).

❉ Listen to your parents and accept their guidance and restrictions (Ephesians 6:1).

❉ Study Scriptures that define sexual sin and use those Scriptures to strengthen your resolve even before the temptation occurs (Luke 4:4, 8, 12).

## TIPS FOR PRETEENS AND YOUNG TEENS

❉ Choose godly friends.

❉ Avoid tempting situations.

❉ Listen to your parents.

❉ Study Scriptures for strength.

❉ Feed your heart pure things.

*Children, obey your parents in the Lord, for this is right* (Ephesians 6:1).

Why is it so difficult for some girls to accept their parents' guidance?

*Keep your heart with all diligence, for out of it spring the issues of life* (Proverbs 4:23).

How can I feed my heart with things that are pure? What things qualify as pure?

*Flee also youthful lusts; but pursue righteousness, faith, love, peace with those who call on the Lord out of a pure heart* (2 Timothy 2:22).

What is the opposite of "fleeing youthful lusts"? Give an example.

❉ Feed your heart things that are pure. Avoid television programs, music, books, and magazines that reduce resistance to sin (Proverbs 4:23).

❉ Stay involved in righteous activities so you have no time or interest to pursue sin (Ephesians 5:18–21; 2 Timothy 2:22).

## LOOKING FOR MR. RIGHT

Arrange the following characteristics by priority in selection of my ideal mate:

___ Personality

___ Intelligence

___ Appearance

___ Ambition

___ Chemistry/Attraction

___ Spirituality

___ Character

___ Creativity

___ Parenting

___ Authenticity (Be Yourself)

**Looking for Mr. Right**

The adage, "every date is a prospective mate," as goofy as it sounds, is actually true. Why would you date someone you would never consider marrying? The majority of Christian women have plans to marry Christian men. So if the adage is correct, they should date Christian men. By not dating Christian men, the Christian woman will have trouble finding a man who has the same values (family, career, priorities) morals (regarding honesty, sex outside of marriage, cheating), and spiritual beliefs (faith, God, salvation). The man who does not follow the path God has set will not be able to raise a family in the discipline and instruction of the Lord (Ephesians 6:4) by being a biblical example of a Christian father and husband. If you decide to date an unsaved person, you need to be open about your faith and ready to teach him the good news of God's plan for salvation. Otherwise, it is best for a Christian female to date only Christian men.

In his book, *Finding the Love of Your Life*, Neil Clark Warren lists 10 characteristics of an ideal spouse. They include personality, intelligence, appearance, ambition, chemistry/attraction, spirituality, character, creativity, parenting, and authenticity (being himself). The more you and your potential date have in common in regard to these ten characteristics, the better your dating experience. Every woman has a mental image of her ideal Mr. Right, and she should never settle for less than her desires. Otherwise she will be unhappy and expect more from her Mr. Wrong than he can give. Remember that dating is not finding the one person you can live with; it is finding the one person you cannot live without. Do not let your fear of never getting married cause you to make the mistake of settling for someone you think you can live with for the rest of your life and not consider what your relationship will be like in the long run. On the flip side, do not mistake infatuation—thinking you cannot live without someone—for the real desire and commitment that time establishes.

**Dating Mr. Right**

Once you have spent a few years waiting, building a big circle of Christian friends (guys and girls), getting to know yourself, and establishing your standards, you may feel ready to date.

Although dating can be a wonderful and fun experience, sometimes couples get carried away with each other and girls can get hurt. Just because you and your date are Christians, that does not mean Satan will not try to tempt you to sin. Girls need to work to protect their hearts. They should be cautious about entering relationships where they grow very attached to a guy and give away emotional pieces of their hearts. They also need to work constantly to guard their own sexual purity.

Just because you and your date are Christians does not mean Satan will not try to tempt you.

## DATING MR. RIGHT

If I really want to date a guy who is not a Christian, do I like him enough to study the Bible with him?

When is the best time to tell my date about my physical boundaries?

If I give in to sexual lusts, how am I different from a non-Christian?

What are the rewards of committing from this day on to pure living?

❧ *Where you go on your date is important.* It is best to go to a public place where other people are present to hold you accountable for your actions. Avoid places that foster inappropriate feelings or actions such as dark rooms, parked cars, or personal places like bedrooms. The darker the location or the more alone a couple is, the more affectionate and passionate they are likely to become. Take advantage of places that include planned activities such as a play, game, or dinner. Then the two of you will not be sitting idle for a long period of time trying to find something to do but end up spending that time "making out."

❧ *Too much affection leads to sexual pro miscuity, a sin in the eyes of God.* Ephesians 5:3 says that even the very hint of sexual immorality is improper for Christians. Of course the Bible does not give exact rules as to how far "too far" is. For example, how long is too long to kiss? Two seconds? Fifteen seconds? Longer? Should you kiss at all? Each Christian should use her discretion and know what is too much for her to handle and cause her to begin sinning with lust. First Peter 1:14–16 states:

As obedient children, not conforming yourselves to the former lusts, as in your ignorance; but as He who called you is holy, you also be holy in all your conduct, because it is written, "Be holy, for I am holy."

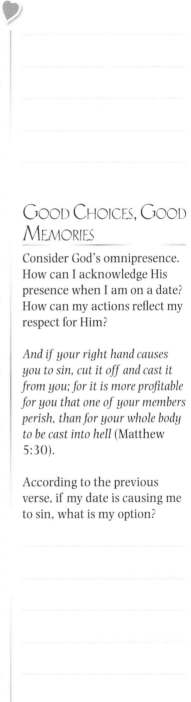

God expects His children to follow Him, so Christians need to be holy in their behavior just as God is holy. In his book, *Sex: It's Worth Waiting For,* George Speck refers to a "moral law of diminishing returns" that states that a couple who has progressed, say, from hugging to kissing cannot return to a less intimate level and be satisfied. The couple has to have more to be satisfied, but then they are never satisfied until they have brought regrettable effects upon friends and family. Remember what Joseph said to Potiphar's wife in Genesis 39:9: "How then can I do this great wickedness, and sin against God?" Joseph knew that sex outside marriage was sin against God.

Okay, so you have waited until you're older and you think you have found Mr. Right. How do you know what he's really all about? This is where dating comes in. Dating is the process of spending time with your potential mate, talking with and learning about him, his beliefs, his goals, and his views of life in general. You have plenty of time to find out whether or not you are compatible. If you are, fabulous! Continue dating to see if that leads you toward a lifelong commitment. If not, that is okay, too. You have learned from the experience more about yourself and what you want in a mate and, hopefully, made a good friend along the way. Dating involves trial and error. It is meeting different Christian men until you find the one without whom you cannot live—Mr. Right.

## Good Choices, Good Memories

The dating years can be some of the most memorable times of the teenage

## GOOD CHOICES, GOOD MEMORIES

Consider God's omnipresence. How can I acknowledge His presence when I am on a date? How can my actions reflect my respect for Him?

*And if your right hand causes you to sin, cut it off and cast it from you; for it is more profitable for you that one of your members perish, than for your whole body to be cast into hell* (Matthew 5:30).

According to the previous verse, if my date is causing me to sin, what is my option?

years. Your choices during these critical years may affect who you ultimately choose to be your lifelong spouse. Even younger girls who are not ready to date can start off on the right foot by hanging around Christian guy friends and getting to know them better. Just remember that dating can be summed up in this: leave room for Jesus. Leave room for Him in your priorities in characteristics of your mate and in affection. When you are out on a date, act as if Christ is there in person eating pizza with you, in the car with you, and beside you at the theater. And when you show affection, pretend He is there also. Therefore, do not engage in any activity that you would be ashamed of doing if God were actually there watching you in person because He is! In accordance with the teachings of Matthew 5:29–30, if your date is causing you to sin, do not date him anymore. Dating is a time for personal and spiritual growth. How much more fun would it be to grow in Christ together—you and your date? Do not give up waiting for Mr. Right.

> If your date is causing you to sin, do not date him anymore.

## Hello, Purity Lover!

**Allison Boyd**

### New and Untouched

I love ice cream. I remember a period of time when my parents consistently purchased Purity ice cream, probably because that brand was on sale. For some reason, it was always important to me that I be the first person to get into the half-gallon box.

In order to break the seal, I would have to rip a piece from the front of the box. "Hello, Purity Lover!" it said underneath in fancy script. I thought it was so much fun to tear away that strip and have the box say hi to me, and then to open the box and be the first one to dig a spoon into that yet un-touched mint chocolate-chip goodness.

One evening, knowing that my mom had been to the store earlier that day, I opened the freezer for my ice cream and was dismayed to find the box already broken into! "Hello Purity Lover!" was visible, but the box was not saying it to me. My mother did not understand why I was upset. "You're not the only one here who likes ice cream," she reminded me. She was right. But it just was not as much fun getting my ice cream out of an already opened box.

There is a natural delight in things new and incorrupt. I've witnessed my brother Tyler, upon opening a jar of peanut but-ter, relish the "ah, fresh peanut butter . . . perfectly smooth and untouched" and then savor the first spoonful. Can you remember the feeling of opening a new box of 64 Cray-ola crayons and knowing it was all yours?

I can't think of an instance when this sensation would be keener than on the wedding night of a man and woman who have kept themselves pure for marriage. God intended sex as a gift: a gift with which He blesses the husband and wife, and as a gift that the husband and wife give to each other. God created sex as a beautiful thing. God even commanded Adam and Eve to "be fruitful, and multiply." Proverbs 5:18–19 says, "Rejoice with the wife of your youth . . . let her breasts satisfy you at all

## HELLO, PURITY LOVER!

Consider the idea of boun-daries: It is not illegal to drive 70 miles per hour on the interstate. But it is illegal to drive that speed downtown. What are God's boundaries in other areas that are not wrong within themselves?

*But fornication and all unclean-ness or covetousness, let it not even be named among you, as is fitting for saints* (Ephesians 5:3).

Ephesians 5:3 states plainly that sex outside marriage is sin. How is it up to me to avoid this sin?

Why do some girls blame this sin on everyone but themselves?

## SEX OUTSIDE OF MARRIAGE

Read Genesis 2. What was God's original intention for sex?

*Do you not know that the unrighteous will not inherit the kingdom of God? Do not be deceived. Neither fornicators, nor idolaters, nor adulterers, nor homosexuals, nor sodomites, nor thieves, nor covetous, nor drunkards, nor revilers, nor extortioners will inherit the kingdom of God. And such were some of you. But you were washed, but you were sanctified, but you were justified in the name of the Lord Jesus and by the Spirit of our God* (1 Corinthians 6:9–11).

Underline "and such were some of you" in 1 Corinthians 6:11. How do these previous verses give hope to one who has committed sexual sin?

Can she stop?

Can she receive cleansing by obeying Christ?

Why should she do this? When?

times"—an obvious reference to the sexual relationship. Why then is sex often viewed so negatively?

**Sex Outside of Marriage**

The Bible says, "Marriage is honorable among all, and the bed undefiled; but fornicators and adulterers God will judge." (Hebrews 13:4). The reason the writer gives for holding marriage in honor is an assurance that God will judge the fornicators and adulterers—those who misuse God's gift. Fornication is any sex outside of a God-approved marriage, and adultery is sexual unfaithfulness in a marriage. God wants His people to enjoy sex within marriage, but He says that sex outside or before marriage is a sin (Ephesians 5:3). People who misuse sex give sex a bad name. Sex itself is intrinsically good—within a God-sanctioned marriage.

We need to remember God's power to forgive. Paul said the Corinthians had involved themselves heavily in sexual sin (1 Corinthians 6:9–10). But then he reminded them that when they obeyed the gospel, "you were washed . . . you were sanctified . . . you were justified in the name of the Lord Jesus" (6:11). If there is sexual sin in your past, commit to having it in your life no more. When we are baptized, God really will forgive us of all our old sins (1 Peter 3:21), and after we are Christians, He hears us when we confess our mistakes and penitently pray for forgiveness (1 John 1:9). Commit to a bright and pure future, and do not let your past keep you from glorifying God with your present!

Sex is like fire. Think of candles, camp-fires, fireworks, and cozy fireplaces. When fire is used carefully, properly, and responsibly, it can bring light, warmth, fun, and comfort. However, when misused or mismanaged, fire can cause great harm: ravaging forest fires, destructive house fires, and painful burn injuries. Outside marriage, sex is both sinful and dangerous.

**For Our Own Good**

God is concerned with our sexual purity because He wants us to enjoy our sexuality as we glorify Him in our bodies. "Whoever commits adultery with a woman lacks understanding; he who does so destroys his own soul" (Proverbs 6:32). Sexual purity is for our own good! Engaging in sex before marriage can lead to pregnancy, disease, loss of self-respect, further sin such as abortion or repeated premarital sex, regret, difficulties in future relationships, and even eternal consequences if we do not repent.

In 1 Corinthians 6:18, Paul explains how sexual sin is different from other sins: "Every sin that a man does is outside the body, but he who commits sexual immorality sins against his own body." Sexual sin hurts us in a way different from every other sin.

As children of God, we should seek to glorify Him in our bodies, as in every area of our lives:

> Do you not know that your bodies are members of Christ? Shall I then take the members of Christ and make them members of a harlot? Certainly not! . . . do you not know that your body is the temple of

## FOR OUR OWN GOOD

Find Scriptures that describe God's temple in the Old Testament. List some adjectives used in the descriptions.

How does my body compare with God's temple of the Old Testament?

What are some ways I can flee sexual immorality (fornication KJV)?

First Corinthians 6:20 states that I am "bought with a price." What was the price tag?

## LESSONS OF THE PAST

Fill in the details of the consequences of both of these Bible characters:

Joseph _____

_____

_____

_____

_____

David _____

_____

_____

_____

_____

David fed his lust and nourished his temptation. How could this happen to me? Why should I study Joseph's method of dealing with temptation?

_____

_____

the Holy Spirit who is in you, whom you have from God, and you are not your own? For you were bought at a price; therefore glorify God in your body and in your spirit, which are God's (1 Corinthians 6:15–20).

We are members of the body of Christ. As such, how can we do anything that Christ Himself would not do? The idea of Jesus committing fornication is ridiculous, and it is equally outrageous for a member of Christ's body to act in that way. "The body is not for sexual immorality but for the Lord," Paul explains in 1 Corinthians 6:13. Because sex outside marriage can hurt us like no other sin, and because we should use our bodies to glorify God, the inspired writer commands Christians to "flee sexual immorality" (1 Corinthians 6:18).

**Lessons of the Past**

The record of Joseph provides a classic example of how God's children should act in the face of sexual temptation:

And it came to pass after these things that his master's wife cast longing eyes on Joseph, and she said, "Lie with me." But he refused and said to his master's wife, "Look, my master does not know what is with me in the house, and he has committed all that he has to my hand. There is no one greater in this house than I, nor has he kept back anything from me but you, because you are his wife. How then can I do this great wickedness, and sin against God?" So it was, as she spoke to Joseph day by day, that he did not heed her, to lie with her or to be with her. But it happened about this time, when Joseph went into the house to do his work, and none of the men of the house was inside, that she caught him by his garment, saying, "Lie with me." But he left his garment in her hand, and fled and ran outside. And so it was, when she saw that he had left his garment in her hand and fled outside (Genesis 39:7–13).

Joseph recognized fornication as a sin against the Lord, and so refused to even be with the woman who was tempting him. At the crucial moment, Joseph actually ran away.

Contrast Joseph's actions with that of David's:

> It happened . . . at the time when kings go out to battle, that David sent Joab and his servants with him, and all Israel . . . But David remained at Jerusalem. Then it happened one evening that David arose from his bed and walked on the roof of the king's house. And from the roof he saw a woman bathing, and the woman was very beautiful to behold. So David sent and inquired about the woman. And someone said, "Is this not Bathsheba, the daughter of Eliam, the wife of Uriah the Hittite?" Then David sent messengers, and took her; and she came to him, and he lay with her . . . And the woman conceived; so she sent and told David, and said, "I am with child" (2 Samuel 11:1–5).

Several factors contributed to David's sin. David chose to remain at Jerusalem "at the time when kings go out to battle." There is no evidence that David sinned by staying home. It was in his leisure time that David ran into temptation. "And from the roof he saw a woman bathing, and the woman was very beautiful to behold." David could have looked away or he could have come down from the roof

It was in his leisure time that David ran into temptation.

# FLEE!

*Sin will take you further than
  you intended to go.
Sin will keep you longer than you
  intended to stay.
Sin will cost you more than you
  intended to pay!*
—Unknown

Do I think "this can't happen to me; I'm a good Christian and I don't take part in such!" What about "Christians" who look at pornographic material; what about those who dabble in the lottery; what about those who dress immodestly not giving a thought that they can cause someone to lust; what about those who are involved in adultery and fornication, or religious error? Can these take me further than I want to go, keep me longer than I want to stay, and cost me more than I want to pay? Yes! And they might even cost me my soul!

Find a verse that advises me to take heed when I think I am standing—I just might fall!

to a less morally dangerous situation. But David fed his lust: he nourished his temptation instead of rejecting it. Scripture says he "inquired about the woman." His very next step was to send for Bathsheba and sleep with her.

### Flee!

In 2 Timothy 2:22, Paul instructs Timothy to flee youthful lusts. A good way to flee temptation is to pursue good things contrary to the sin we are tempted to commit. We should pursue purity in our thoughts, words, and actions.

> But each one is tempted when he is drawn away by his own desires and enticed. Then, when desire has conceived, it gives birth to sin; and sin, when it is full-grown, brings forth death. Do not be deceived, my beloved brethren (James 1:14–16).

The way to avoid being enticed to sin is to avoid lust! God urges us not to be deceived by our own desires. In fact, Jesus taught that lust is equivalent to adultery (Matthew 5:27–28). While men and boys struggle more with lust as a result of visual stimulation, women and girls often lust because we think too much! Excessive daydreaming and fantasizing can lead to unhealthy obsession. If our daydreaming includes impure thoughts, that daydreaming is especially dangerous.

### A Faithful Guard

Proverbs 4:23 says, "Keep your heart with all diligence, for out of it spring the issues of life." Things that happen first in our hearts will directly affect our life-alter-

ing choices! In order to keep our thoughts pure, we should guard our hearts. Would a faithful guard knowingly admit the enemy? Of course not! Neither should we allow Satan's influence to enter our minds through the movies we watch, music we listen to, pictures we look at, or books and magazines we read. Once we let a sinful image or scenario enter our minds and hearts, it is difficult to completely make it go away! Paul, inspired by the Holy Spirit, tells us not to give place to the devil (Ephesians 4:27). Psalm 101:3 says, "I will set nothing wicked before my eyes."

When talking with members of the opposite sex, it is sometimes easy to say things we do not mean in order to promote a guy's interest. Proverbs 7:21 describes a woman seducing a man with "enticing speech" and "with her flattering lips." Our motives and conversation should be kept pure! Flirting is no exception to this rule. Remember, "it is shameful even to speak of those things which are done by them in secret" (Ephesians 5:12). Friendliness and genuine interest in another person are good, but sexually suggestive speech, even if only mildly suggestive, is wrong.

**Plan Ahead**

Sexual purity is most apparent in our actions, especially in our physical acts of affection when in a relationship with a guy. Proverbs 4:26–27 reads, "Ponder the path of your feet, and let all your ways be established. Do not turn to the right or the left; remove your foot from evil." This passage emphasizes the importance of planning ahead. Decide before the moment of

## A FAITHFUL GUARD

Read the following verses from Psalm 1 and Proverbs 4. Underline the following words: walks, stands, sits, meditates, enter, avoid, travel, turn, and pass. What do all of these words have in common? How can they help me to "take heed and not fall"?

*Blessed is the man who walks not in the counsel of the ungodly, nor stands in the path of sinners, nor sits in the seat of the scornful; but his delight is in the law of the Lord, and in His law he meditates day and night (Psalm 1:1–2).*

*Do not enter the path of the wicked, and do not walk in the way of evil. Avoid it, do not travel on it; turn away from it and pass on (Proverbs 4:14–15).*

What are some examples of sexually suggestive speech?

temptation what you will and will not do with a guy. I will not attempt to draw a line and tell you exactly "how far is too far." If an action provokes lust, it is sinful. You know what causes you to lust. Don't do it!

Galatians 5:19–21 tells us that lasciviousness will keep us from going to heaven. While we don't use this word much anymore, we must understand what it means in order to remain sexually pure. *Lasciviousness* means unchaste handling between males and females. Sexual purity means more than avoiding sex outside marriage. It means avoiding the indecent touching that leads to lustful passion. Sitting in a boy's lap, giving him a massage, or letting him touch us under our clothes are actions that we would be hard pressed to honestly describe as pure.

**Just Say No**

Don't be afraid to say no to something that makes you uncomfortable, even if it's just holding hands. It is possible that something appropriate outside marriage, such as a hug, may be inappropriate at one stage of a relationship and may become appropriate later on. Pay attention to your inhibitions, "for if our heart condemns us, God is greater than our heart, and knows all things" (1 John 3:20). God intends for us to be uncomfortable when we commit actions He forbids.

In addition to considering what causes us to lust or feel uncomfortable, we should consider how our actions will affect the boy we are with. First Thessalonians 4 speaks of sexual immorality as defrauding or wronging a brother. When a man and woman

## Plan Ahead

If girls really know what leads to lust but they do it anyway, how can they be pure?

What are my own standards about purity and touching in the context of dating? What will I do or not do?

How can I know "how far is too far" regarding physical acts of affection?

## Just Say "No"

Why does a girl sometimes feel pressure to say yes to physical affection that really makes her feel uncomfortable?

"It is the young woman's responsibility to draw the line regarding physical contact." How do you feel about that statement?

engage in sexual sin, they sin against one another. In effect, they steal from one another, as well as from their future spouses. Have you ever opened a Christmas present, only to find pieces broken or missing? The effect of premarital unfaithfulness is the same.

May we all cherish our sexual purity—for our Creator, for ourselves, and for our possible future mate. "Hel-lo-o-o, purity lover!"

## Works Cited

Speck, George. *Sex: It's Worth Waiting For*. Chicago: Moody Publishers, 1989.

McDonald, Cleveland, and Philip M. McDonald. *Creating a Successful Christian Marriage*. 4th ed. Grand Rapids: Baker Book House, 1994.

Warren, Neil Clark. *Finding the Love of Your Life: Ten Principles for Choosing the Right Marriage Partner*. New York: Pocket Books, 1992.

# NOTES

# CHAPTER TWELVE

# Dressing for Spiritual Success — What the Guys Say

### Allison Boyd

## One-Track Mind

What girl in her right mind wants to be around a guy who is interested only in sex? What Christian girl is pleased when guys make sexually suggestive comments, touch her inappropriately, or too obviously stare at her body? Christian girls are disappointed by a guy's crude behavior. We ever bewail this misplaced emphasis. Good news, girls. There is something we can do!

The following comments are taken from a survey of Christian guys, ages 14 to 24.

❉ "It is important that you realize there are young men struggling in ways you can't understand."

❉ "I do not think that most girls understand the thoughts that go through men's heads when they see a girl dressed the way she shouldn't be—or she definitely would not dress that way."

## ONE-TRACK MIND

Ask some older women to recommend books for girls that will increase their understanding of how guys think. Share these recommendations with the class.

Regarding my clothes—what reaction do others have to the clothes I wear? (Staring at neckline, etc.)

❖ "Boys certainly view what girls wear differently from the way girls view what other girls wear."

❖ "Guys are weak in this area. Immodest dress doesn't help us out."

❖ "I would love to tell all Christian girls that they have an enormous power and influence over Christian men simply by the way they dress."

❖ "I do not believe the average girl understands how much of a problem lust causes for the average guy. For the most part, this lust is visual."

❖ "Whether girls realize it or not, their clothes can be a problem. A true Christian sister will consider how her dress will affect her Christian brothers."

### Don't Be a Hypocrite

Surveys have revealed that many Christian men wish girls would respect guys enough to dress more tastefully and modestly. These are the pleas of our brothers! It is hypocritical for us to complain about guys' preoccupation with sex when we, whether knowingly or unknowingly, contribute to the problem.

Do we love our brothers in Christ and the other men around us? Read 1 Corinthians 13. Among other things, the inspired writer says that love "does not parade itself, is not puffed up; does not behave rudely, does not seek its own" (1 Corinthians 13:4–5). Does Paul describe our attitude toward the guys in our lives? If we love them, we care for their souls and will do anything to help them spiritually.

> As women's clothing gets tighter and reveals more skin, it becomes easier for men to sin.

No girl, by dressing immodestly, forces a guy to lust. Men have a choice. But as women's clothing gets tighter and reveals more skin, it becomes easier for men to sin. Lust is a sin (Romans 13:13), and we do not want to cause others to stumble by tempting them to harbor impure thoughts (Romans 14:13). Certainly no Christian lady wants to be guilty of dressing just immodestly enough to push someone over the edge. Rather, we should "bear one another's burdens, and so fulfill the law of Christ" (Galatians 6:2).

**Tight Clothes, Too Much Skin, Visible Undergarments**

What constitutes modesty? The Christian young men surveyed agreed that low-cut shirts and thin see-through garments (without additional clothing underneath) are unquestionably immodest. Other responses varied because each man's personal temptation is different. Sixty-five percent said that shirts that reveal a girl's lower back when she sits are immodest. Over 75 percent agreed that tight shirts were immodest. "Tight clothing, especially," one Christian guy says, "produces more impure thoughts within a man's head than girls will ever know." The majority rated tight jeans as immodest. Nearly half the Christian men surveyed said that "skirts above knee" are immodest, with an identical rating for "shorts above knee."

Over 70 percent of survey participants agreed that thin or see-through garments with additional clothing underneath are acceptable, provided the clothing underneath is modest. One respondent explained, con-

## Don't Be a Hypocrite

Teacher's Note: Consider having your girls host their own "Girls' Only" fashion show outside of class. Or, have them bring in magazine pictures of girls modeling different outfits. Use the opportunity to discuss modesty in clothes.

How can I "bear another's burdens" by the way I dress?

## Tight Clothes, Too Much Skin, Visible Undergarments

What are some ideas for looking pretty without drawing unnecessary attention to my body?

cerning see-through clothing that it "depends on which part is see-through (such as arms)." Another participant wondered if just being able to see through something a girl is wearing might be enough to cause a guy to lust, regardless of what is or is not underneath.

The same percentage of Christian guys surveyed said that sleeveless shirts are modest. However, several were unsure on this question. One young man implied that spaghetti-strap shirts are immodest; another said sleeveless shirts are modest, "except tank-tops." Another survey respondent said sleeveless shirts "can be both." A few rated sleeveless shirts as altogether immodest, expressing concern over the visibility of girls' underarms.

Christian young men are in wide agreement that visible undergarments indicate immodesty. "Thongs are bad," one survey respondent declares. "I don't want to see that," says another guy. Another elaborates, "Yes, guys laugh at you when that short shirt shows your underwear." These statistics provide us with much-needed insight as to how our brothers view us in light of the clothes we wear.

## EYE–OPENER EXERCISES

* *Eye-opener skirt test:* Sit in front of a full length mirror and cross your legs. Does the skirt have enough material?

* *Eye-opener shirt test:* Stand in front of a full length mirror. Now lean forward as if to pick up some object. Is your shirt or blouse modest?

* *Eye-opener midriff test:* Stand in front of a full length mirror. Reach up with both arms above your head. Do your shirt and pants overlap? They should.

**Ask the Guys**

What does the way a girl dresses reveal about her character? Here is what some guys had to say:

* "You can tell by the way a girl wears her clothes if she is 'loose' or not."

* "Maturity and responsibility are revealed in a girl's choice of clothes."

❊ "Clothes reflect how seriously she takes herself, her Christianity, and any relationships she might be in."

❊ "Her priorities and the beauty she values are easily spotted by her dress."

❊ "If she wants to be noticed because of her body, it is a spiritual turn off."

❊ "What she wears tells whether she is boastful or humble."

❊ "You can tell by what she wears what she wants guys to think about when they look at her."

❊ "Her clothes show how much she respects herself and how much she wants to be respected."

❊ "I know how a girl expects to be treated when I see what she's wearing."

❊ "Her clothes tell if she carefully considers and applies the practical implications of God's Word."

❊ "Girls who show a lot of skin are usually trashy."

❊ "Girls who wear immodest clothes will not appear to be Christians."

❊ "I believe a girl professes true godliness when she takes the time to find modest clothes and seeks to dress in a way so as not to be a stumbling block."

### ASK THE GUYS

What motivates girls to dress with less?

What Scriptures give principles to help us decide how to dress?

**Shop Smart**

Often when they shop, girls ask each other, "Is this okay?" or "Is this immodest?" We know that it is easier to agree that clothes are "okay" or not blatantly immodest than to agree that they are actually modest. Too often, we are motivated by a

## SHOP SMART

How often do I shop for items that will improve my spiritual beauty?

What scripture defines true spiritual beauty?

How does the time I spend on improving my spiritual beauty compare with the time I spend improving my physical beauty? (To make this comparison, keep accurate records of both activities for a week.)

## THE INSIDE IS FOREVER

Dorcas was described as being "full of good works and charitable deeds." How was her spirit valued more than her appearance?

## THE SWIMSUIT ISSUE

How can I enjoy the beach or the water without dressing immodestly and without surrounding myself with other people wearing practically no clothes?

worldly desire to be pretty rather than to display a spirit of humility, love for our brothers, and a desire to please God. We try to rationalize our clothing choices as "okay," "not immodest," or "modest enough," but girls, the guys are smarter than we credit them. They see right through us. When shopping, we should first consider what is modest and then select from the modest what is pretty.

"To me, it shows selfishness," one brother says of immodesty. "It's the attitude 'I want to look good; I don't care what happens to my brothers in Christ,' no matter what the girl may say otherwise."

The time has come for us girls to update our closets! Sheila Butt writes:

> Take good, long, honest looks in the mirror. Look in your closet. Look at pictures of yourself. Reevaluate your wardrobe. I often tell young ladies that if something is not on sale, they should not advertise it. Women who are seeking spiritual beauty will be advertising their goodness by the way they dress. What are the women in your family advertising? Are you showing the world that you are seeking spiritual beauty? (*Seeking Spiritual Beauty*, p. 25).

**The Inside Is Forever**

Passages such as 1 Timothy 2:9–10 and 1 Peter 3:3–4 reveal that a woman's spirit is of more value to the Lord than her outward appearance. We should have this attitude as well! The world tells us that outward beauty is integral to our worth, but God tells us otherwise! "It's not about looks," one Christian brother agrees. "If you are beautiful on the inside then you are beautiful on the outside."

It is very true that guys are concerned with physical attraction to a girl—how she looks. But any girl can attract guys' attention when she is wearing immodest clothing. A truly beautiful girl, however, is one who is beautiful on the inside as well as the outside—and she shows this by wearing modest clothing.

Notice more comments from guys about modesty:

❁ "Dress is the first thing I notice about a girl. If she is wearing something too low or too tight, I'm not interested!"

❁ "There is nothing better than a girl who dresses modestly. Then she knows guys are attracted to her and not her body."

❁ "If you want to be attractive, try revealing the hidden person of the heart which has the imperishable quality of a gentle and quiet spirit. To me, that is attractive."

**The Swimsuit Issue**

"Look to the Bible for instruction," one young man advises. The Bible tells us to dress modestly, but it does not give explicit rules concerning dress. The Bible's words about preserving sexual purity, helping others avoid sin, demonstrating self-respect, and being an example to the world should help us to determine a reasonable standard for what is pure to wear. Let's make this practical.

What about swimsuits? Even one-piece swimsuits reveal all of our legs, much of

## CHRISTIAN GUYS SPEAK OUT

❁ "Just like good girls are not impressed by a guy showing off and trying to act tough to gain a girl's attention, good guys are not impressed by a girl's dressing immodestly to gain attention."

❁ "Plain and simple: The kinds of guys that are going to be attracted to immodestly dressed Christian girls are not the kinds of guys that Christian girls should be looking for."

❁ "Guys that are actually trying to find a good Christian woman are begging to find . . . one that exemplifies her godliness in her actions, mindset, and even dress."

❁ "Your Christianity should shine through in every aspect of your life, including dress."

❁ "Dress modestly. We dig it."

❁ "Try to be as modest as possible. It will help other girls (Christian or not)."

❁ "Being a Christian means being different."

❁ "Always remember who you are and how you stand for the name of Jesus . . . Never, ever prohibit yourself from showing His righteous name."

our backs, and part of our chests. Since they cling to us so tightly, they clearly reveal our figures to any onlookers. Girls, is this pure? Is it decent? Will it help men keep their thoughts clean? Surely we can be consistent enough to understand that if our brothers tell us that low-cut shirts and tight jeans cause them to stumble, then a tight, wet outfit that covers barely more than our underwear won't help them stay pure either! Both one-piece and two-piece swimsuits are immodest. (Of course, swimsuits may be worn among members of the same sex.) Like any other form of immodesty, "mixed swimming"—mature males and females wearing swimsuits in each other's company—is a stumbling block to others.

One guy emphasized: "I do not for a moment believe swimsuits are modest. If they are, why do guys rush to buy the *Sports Illustrated Swimsuit Issue;* and why do they claim they watch the Victoria's Secret fashion show for their live musical bands?"

Let us strive to be consistent in our standards for modesty. Not only does God expect us to be modest, but our Christian brothers desire it as well! How encouraging!

> Not only does God expect us to be modest, but our Christian brothers do, too.

**Recommended reading:**

Butt, Sheila. *Seeking Spiritual Beauty.* Huntsville, AL: Publishing Designs, Inc, 2002.

# Dancing Out of Step

## Hannah Colley

Dancing—something the whole world glorifies. In the enchanting movie, *White Christmas*, Danny Kaye sang: "The best things happen when you're dancing." Whitney Houston belted it out in her song: "I Wanna Dance with Somebody." Fred Astaire once sang, "You can take my breakfast, you can take my lunch, you can take my women, but if swing goes, I go too." It's just a wholesome activity for everyone—or is it? Consider this chapter your personal dancing lesson. Then you can decide for yourself whether or not dancing is for you.

**What Is Dancing?**

Dictionary.com defines it "to move rhythmically, usually to music, using prescribed or improvised steps and gestures." Dancing can be a party activity, a hobby, or a sport. It can be done alone or with one person of the same or opposite sex or with several people. It always involves some sort of movement of the body. People of all ages are involved in dancing.

So what's the big deal? How can something so widely accepted be wrong? I admit I have struggled with this question. Some forms of dancing are pure, clean fun. We know this not only by using our common sense, but also by reading biblical examples.

## WHAT IS DANCING?

"Thou shalt not dance," is not in the Bible. How can I determine what God wants of me?

My definition of dancing:

## WHAT DOES THE BIBLE SAY?

Define *lasciviousness* in your own words.

*For from within, out of the heart of [girls], proceed evil thoughts, adulteries, fornications, murders, thefts, covetousness, wickedness, deceit, lewdness, an evil eye, blasphemy, pride, foolishness. All these evil things come from within and defile a [girl]* (Mark 7:21–23).

Mark 7:21–23 tells me what happens to girls who behave wickedly. Why do I need to avoid this behavior?

### LASCIVIOUS GIRL

Madonna's song, *Material Girl*, is full of empty words reflecting worldliness. Find the lyrics to that song, and substitute "lascivious" for "material" and read aloud. Do you think this rendition is accurate?

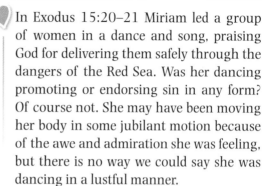 In Exodus 15:20–21 Miriam led a group of women in a dance and song, praising God for delivering them safely through the dangers of the Red Sea. Was her dancing promoting or endorsing sin in any form? Of course not. She may have been moving her body in some jubilant motion because of the awe and admiration she was feeling, but there is no way we could say she was dancing in a lustful manner.

This chapter is about the kind of dancing that goes on at your high school or middle school dance.

### What Does the Bible Say?

Chances are you probably didn't know the Bible condemns dancing. In fact, you may have even used that as an argument in favor of dancing. Several of my friends have said, "Nowhere in the Bible does it say, 'Thou shalt not dance.'" What I am about to show you may surprise you.

Note the words of the apostle Paul:

> Now the works of the flesh are evident, which are: adultery, fornication, uncleanness, lewdness, idolatry, sorcery, hatred, contentions, jealousies, outbursts of wrath, selfish ambitions, dissensions, heresies, envy, murders, drunkenness, revelries, and the like; of which I tell you beforehand, just as I also told you in time past, that those who practice such things will not inherit the kingdom of God (Galatians 5:19–21).

Look at the word *lasciviousness*. This may be the first time you have heard this word. It is not often that, when we go on a date, our moms say to us as we walk out the door: "Have a good time and don't be lascivious!" So what did God mean by that word? The Greek word for lasciviousness is *aselgeia*. According to Thayer's Greek lexicon, one of the definitions of *aselgeia* is "wanton manners as filthy words, indecent bodily movements, unchaste handling of males and females." Read that definition again. What does that remind you of? It should remind you of the prom, the seventh-grade dance, and the homecoming dance.

## Hormones and Music

I talked with one mom recently who was upset about what had gone on at her son's middle-school dance. Her son came home and told her that there were seventh and eighth graders committing fornication in the corners of the gym while the dance was going on. She could not believe that such would happen at such a prestigious and academically upstanding school. I hate to be blunt, but when you fill a gym with pre-teens and teens, turn the lights down low, and encourage them to rub their bodies against each other to the slow rhythm of seductive music, what do you expect? If it isn't a slow song, it's an upbeat one where one will move his or her body in front of his or her partner while that partner looks on and does the same. Call me radical, but if the kind of dancing that goes on at the prom and other such dances is not "unchaste handling of males and females indecent bodily movement," I am interested to know what is. Frankly, I cannot think of anything that better fits the description "indecent bodily movement" than modern-day dancing does.

Lascivious—aselgeia (Gr.): Wanton manners, filthy words, indecent bodily movements, unchaste handling of males and females.

## Hormones and Music

Think about the bodily movements of the modern dance. Can you imagine Christ moving His body in such a way?

When is it acceptable to dance with a guy?

In the above passage, Galatians 5:19–21, God does not just say, "Try to avoid these things." He says, "Those who practice such things will not inherit the kingdom of God." I don't know about you, but I don't want to risk my salvation over a few school dances. It is really not worth it.

Another part of that passage that catches my eye is the words: "and the like." That means that, as a Christian, I should stay as far from the sins listed in this passage as possible. In today's society, what (besides dancing) might involve lasciviousness? The way we dress, our dating behavior, the CDs we listen to, and the movies we watch can all cause us to be lascivious. Please remember the definition of lascivious as you reflect on those things in other chapters of this book.

**Is This Dancing, Too?**

One form of dancing is difficult for me to discuss because it is so popular, even among many Christians. It is called cheerleading. I realize that those in every school are not guilty, but in most cases, cheerleading is a lascivious activity. The skirts come far above the knee and they come up frequently during flips, cartwheels, and the like, to reveal what is no more modest than skimpy underwear. There is usually a tease line between the skirt and top, and sometimes the entire stomach is revealed. I don't have to tell you this. You know. Not only are these girls extremely immodest, but most of their movements are lascivious. The movements go anywhere from swinging hips to shaking chests, but these movements are provoking lust in the op-

posite sex, whether we girls realize it or
not. In a way, cheerleading is worse than
dancing. At dances, a girl moves her body
in front of one guy. At the ball games, a girl
moves her body in front of a large crowd
as a form of entertainment. Girls, what are
we thinking!

Please don't misunderstand me. I think
cheering for your favorite team is a wonderful thing to do, but we can cheer just as
well with all of our clothes on and without
indecent movements. Perhaps, most of the
time, we will just have to cheer from the
bleachers instead of in front of the crowd!

**What Will I Do?**

Once you know what lasciviousness
is, and once you have really thought in
the light of that definition about dancing,
you have to decide whether or not to participate. There is no straddling the fence.
Yes, you will be different, or even weird,
because you do not involve yourself in
the activities of your friends, but it will be
worth it. Standing up for what you believe
will help you grow by leaps and bounds.
But that is not the best part. The best part
is that you will be rewarded one day for the
stand you take now, and you will be glad
you took that stand!

Doing right takes lots of sacrifice. I
have tried to talk several of my friends out
of going to the prom, and I always hear the
words: "You only get one chance to go to
your senior prom."

That's true, but let's look at the flip
side. You only get one chance to stand up
and say no to your senior prom. That's all.
After you have gone to the prom—or any

## IS THIS DANCING, TOO?

Brainstorm with Christian
friends about ways to help
cheerleading comply with
God's standards—in dress and
movement.

What is a good, biblical reason
for cheerleading outfits to be
short and skimpy?

other dance, for that matter—you will never have that chance again. You will never be able to sacrifice that particular special evening for the one who sacrificed His own life for you. Christianity is meant to be a sacrifice. Romans 12:1–2 says,

> I beseech you therefore, brethren, by the mercies of God, that you present your bodies a living sacrifice, holy, acceptable to God, which is your reasonable service. And do not be conformed to this world, but be transformed by the renewing of your mind, that you may prove what is that good and acceptable and perfect will of God.

I beg you to consider seriously your views on dancing, remembering what the Bible says about dancing and, as Christian girls, let's show our true colors by not participating therein.

## WHAT WILL I DO?

What is a good, biblical reason for attending a senior prom or other dance?

What sacrifices am I presenting to God with my body?

Dear Girls,

We hope that this study has benefited you as much as preparing it has benefited us. We are humbled by the opportunity to present these lessons because we struggle with these issues ourselves. Our goal is to apply biblical principles to specific situations in our lives. We urge you to reflect on this study with an open Bible and an open heart.

Living in Christ is more than following a checklist of rules. Your actions should be a natural outgrowth of your love for God and desire to obey Him.

Our prayer is that together we will all grow to be more Christ-like. We hope and pray that you will become the mature Christian that God would have you to be. We may never meet many of you in this lifetime, but we love you, and we all want to be in heaven together!

Love,

Genevieve  Lora  Heather A.
Lyndsay  Laura  Allison
Hannah  Heather B.

# NOTES